The
SHINING
LIGHT

THE MAN, MISSION, AND MOVEMENT
OF THE YMCA

DR. DAVID NEWMAN

with HEIDI S. MULLER

"The YMCA began because a group of friends believed that the teachings and example of Jesus could heal their world. Their gatherings launched an association that echoes across time, inviting all who seek belonging, rest, and re-creation to gather among friends. This book captures the transformational impact that the light had on the YMCA's founder and on the movement known as the YMCA."

JORGE PEREZ
President & CEO | YMCA Of Greater Cincinnati

"After serving the YMCA movement for more than twenty five years as a volunteer, I cannot thank God enough for this book that will help us to recover our tremendous, relevant, and empowering Spiritual Heritage, rooted in the love of God, that brings transformation in the lives of young men and women in this hurting world. I urge you to read it with an open mind and join thousands of the YMCA community committed to serving humanity."

CAESAR K. L. MOLEBATSI
Past President | World Alliance of YMCAs

"Dr. David Newman is arguably the most educated person in the world on the history and mission of the YMCA. He shares with us the aims and values of our YMCA founder and also gives us practical insight on how to further them in contemporary YMCA contexts. This book will be helpful to YMCAs all across the world, especially as they re-imagine what their YMCA will look like post—COVID 19."

JOSHUA HEASTON
Director of Christian Mission
YMCA of Greater Indianapolis

"When the YMCA started back in 1844, it did not grow slowly but instead it spread like a wildfire across the land, across oceans into the cities and into the boroughs all over the world. It was the power of God's love that started the organization, through one 19-year-old, who out of his love for God, wanted to share that love to all those around him!

This book is a testimony to the YMCA and what it can be at its very best, when we intentionally infuse the organization with the "touch of the Master's hand". The combination of the YMCA history and personal stories of YMCA leaders who led not by their own power, but His, is inspiring. David Newman beautifully captures the true essence of one of the greatest human service organizations on the planet, by teaching us to be faithful to the intent of those who went before us."

ERIC ELLSWORTH
CEO | YMCA of the Cayman Islands

"Dr. Newman has done a remarkable job with this book. The time has come for the Young Men's Christian Association, the YMCA, the Y to fulfill its God-given potential. This book is a call to all YMCA leaders—both staff and volunteers, that on our watch we will remember our identity, both individually and as a movement, is in Christ. We will tell. We will stand. We will serve. We will pray. We will act in such a way as to usher in His Kingdom. It's gonna be amazing!"

ANGELA PRENGER
CEO | Long Branch Area YMCA | Macon, Missouri

"I deeply believe the YMCA should be leaning into our Christian history, legacy, and mission as the source of our compassion, love, and care for all. We need the lessons, reminders, stories, and examples shared in this book to remind us who we are and to embolden us to reach for what we are still called to be."

CHRIS JOHNSON
President and CEO
Countryside YMCA | Lebanon, Ohio

"Over the past decade I have learned more about the history and mission of the YMCA from Dr. David Newman than any other single source. To now have his expertise and passion come together in this little book is an absolute treasure. May it inspire and embolden scores of YMCA workers and movements around the globe as it has done for me."

REV. BJORN D. DIXON
YMCA of the North and the WHY Church | Minnesota

"David Newman's historical account is a compelling love story of the life of Sir George Williams. Written in first person as Newman traces his journey from the remote rural farm of Williams' childhood to iconic locations in London that inspired the beginning of the YMCA. Newman uncovers the 'first principle': faith in Jesus Christ and love for our neighbors, based from Scripture: Matthew 22: 34-40; that ignited a small group of young men to launch a global movement known as the Young Men's Christian Association. During recovery from a COVID world, this is a most timely read, not only to commemorate the bicentennial of George Williams' birth, but to reconnect with the 'original DNA' that nourished strong roots to foster sustainable growth."

NORRIS D. LINEWEAVER | Director General (Retired)
Jerusalem International YMCA
Immediate Past President
World Fellowship of YMCA Retirees

ABOUT THE AUTHORS

DAVID NEWMAN

David loves the YMCA and has a passion to lift the C in this movement. He pastors a church that is partnered with his local Y and he has a life-long vision of seeing a church partnered with each of the 14,000 YMCAs around the world. David has had the opportunity to experience the mission in amazing ways as he has helped to build many YMCAs in remote parts of the world. Most importantly, David loves God, his amazing wife, and his four sons. They live in Lebanon, Ohio where he serves on the board of the Countryside YMCA. Every year he hopes the Packers will win the Super Bowl, The Red Sox will win the World Series, Cornell will win the Ivy league (in lacrosse), and Auburn will win the national championship (or at least beat Bama).

HEIDI S. MULLER

Heidi is a collaborative writer who helps boots-on-the-ground ministry leaders to share their vision, expertise and stories. Her passion is to see grace and truth spoken to the church and culture. Heidi helps to lead a college Bible study near Kent State University campus, and some of her greatest joys are teaching the Bible and discipling women. (She also loves hanging out with her big family, listening to live music, and eating dark chocolate.)

ACKNOWLEDGEMENTS

It's a joy to say thank you to a few people who have meant so much to me on this journey.

To my church family: Anchored in God's Word. Full of the Spirit's power. Willing to give up the flashy "church show" to be on mission at the YMCA. Antioch, we are living our namesake.

I love our church!

To the team at India Gospel League:
Mallory: You are an administrative ninja.
Kris: You took on a design project that you said had the craziest time frame you have ever even heard of! I love being in the crazy with you.

To Heidi: You took my thoughts, ideas, and stories and helped me write with clarity and strength. You coached, encouraged, and made everything better. I can't wait for you to one day see the fruit of your labor. Thank you, my friend!

To Pete and Robin: Thank you for editing this book with skill and wisdom.

To Robert: Awesome illustrations. God used you, man.

To Dave: Thank you for being a catalyst in the Kingdom of God.

To Chris, my CEO/friend: Thank you for leading Countryside YMCA with the true mission before us.

To Spence: You put the stake in the ground and said, "Our Y will forever be anchored on faith." Your grandpa would be proud. Your neighbor is too.

To my parents, my in-laws, and my three "glorious brothers": Thank you for shaping me.

To my four sons: Passionate and bold. Lovers of Jesus. Leaders of men. Shaking up the world. I am so proud of you. We will easily throw down 100+ wings as we watch a Packer game.

And to Ashli: You are the most beautiful, powerful person I know.

I love you forever.

TABLE OF CONTENTS

This book is dedicated to the thousands of YMCA employees around the world. You work long hours, get paid very little and sacrifice greatly for the beautiful mission to which you have pledged your lives. Thank you for coaching kids, cleaning gyms, serving orphans, counseling at camps, mentoring the next generation, and putting the love of Christ on display!

All proceeds from this book will go to furthering the Christian mission of the YMCA around the world.

Arise, shine, for your light has come,
    and the glory of the LORD has risen upon you.
For behold, darkness shall cover the earth,
    and thick darkness the peoples;
but the LORD will arise upon you,
    and his glory will be seen upon you.
And nations shall come to your light,
    and kings to the brightness of your rising.

—Isaiah 60:1-3 ESV

FORWARD

A few years ago I walked along the streets of London with a group of YMCA leaders as David Newman diligently and passionately traced the early years of George Williams and the founding of the first YMCA. It is with the same gripping passion that he narrates the history and spiritual roots of the movement in this book.

From the first meetings in a factory bunk room to the global reach of the YMCA today, this movement has always been a people's movement for transformation. Today the YMCA holds that same great potential for impacting individuals, communities, and even nations. Yes, the YMCA has this potential. But will it live up to it?

I am honored to have been asked to write a foreword to this short but significant work. The very timing of this writing is amazing: it is the bicentennial birthday of George Williams and a pivotal point in the history of the YMCA movement. Our world has witnessed rapid and drastic changes in every realm of life over recent decades. Now we find ourselves standing at a crossroads, eager to take the next step. While a glimpse into the future is promising and exciting, it also seems disturbingly perilous. There are tremendous opportunities to grow, to reach out, and to impact the world around us. At the same time, across the globe, youth grapple with uncertainty, upheaval, and increasing cynicism.

This defining moment calls for a good measure of courage to say yes, as well as the courage to say no. It requires boldness to make the right choices, the right decisions, and the sacrifices that those choices and decisions will demand of us.

Those years ago, when David and I walked through the streets of London, a central question emerged. "What if?" "What if every single one of the fourteen thousand local YMCAs became a lighthouse for the transforming love of God? How can we make that happen?" Since that day, David and I have met quite often, along with other global YMCA leaders, to discuss that very question. We have met in Lebanon, Ohio; we have met in Salem, India; we have met in many other cities around the world. Without exaggeration I can say that every single one of our conversations directly or indirectly has revolved around that singular question—"What if?"—and ways and means to realize that passionate vision.

This book invites readers to reflect on the life and person of the young man who launched the YMCA all those years ago. We are celebrating him today not because he was extraordinarily charismatic, uniquely intellectual, or supremely gifted but because George Williams was a loving man and a faithful man, confident in the mission with which he believed God had entrusted him. From his faithful stewardship launched a movement which transforms lives even today.

We stand at a crossroads. Will we, like George Williams, move forward, faithful and confident in the mission upon which the YMCA was founded? Will we grow and thrive, alive with the heartbeat of God's transforming love? Or will we stagnate, institutionalize, and busy ourselves maintaining a machine? What will we choose?

"This is what the LORD says: 'Stand at the crossroads and look; ask for the ancient paths, ask where the good way is, and walk in it, and you will find rest for your souls'" (Jer. 6:16 NIV). The prophet Jeremiah wrote this thousands of years ago, but his message is equally relevant today. I feel certain that those involved in the YMCA will agree that our great movement is indeed at a crossroads. Amid competing ideas, crashing tensions, and a variety of attractive ideologies, there is no need to panic or go astray. Before us lies a well-trodden "ancient path," one confidently walked by George Williams, Dwight Moody, Oswald Chambers, and thousands of other faithful men and women.

This path is a good way! It is a way that leads to soul rest for a weary world.

My prayer is that this book would point back to that path and then guide us forward along it.

> Dr. Samuel D. Stephens, DMin
> President of India Gospel League
> Former Deputy President of the World Alliance
> of YMCAs | Salem, India
> July 2021

INTRODUCTION

Almost two centuries ago twelve friends crammed together in a tiny dorm room above a factory where they worked, slept, and lived. They were dirty, exhausted, and depleted. Like countless other young men, they were in the shadow of the machine that drove nineteenth-century industrialization in London. Once hopeful and naive, their generation was hardening, losing sight of purpose, and experiencing a great soul-weariness.

At first glance these twelve young men would seem like any other group of factory laborers: in their teens and early twenties, poor, hungry. There was something different, however, about the men gathered in room 14 that day. Their hearts were aflame with the excitement of change. They were bound by the discovery of a hope that would bring light to the darkness of their times. They were part of a story that originated in the very heart of God.

There was something different about this little group of men in room 14, and there was something different about the young man who had invited them there. George

Williams, a farm kid turned factory laborer, was driving the conversation, excitement, and direction. Friends said he "radiated joy and enthusiasm."[1] He was convinced that the truth which had transformed his own life would answer the heartache of his times.

Sensing that God was leading them, George and his friends chose a name for their tiny movement: the Young Men's Christian Association. They could never have imagined the rays of light that would move out of that dorm room and shine into industrial London and then into the world.

———————

Fifty-six years later this dorm room prayer meeting had miraculously become a movement that was bursting across the globe. The year was 1900, and YMCA leaders gathered together in Saint Petersburg, Russia, to answer a single question: What should we call ourselves?

They wanted to represent the mission and the heart of the movement in a way that would resonate with their communities. Clearly, the English acronym YMCA would not do.

After some deliberation and debate, they chose a single word: Mayak.[2] *Mayak* is the Russian word for "lighthouse."

In the fiercest storm, a lighthouse provides a flash of hope.

To a lost sailor, a lighthouse gives clear direction.

In the darkest night, the light shines in the darkness, and the darkness cannot overcome it.

I wonder if these leaders could ever have imagined a day when there would be more than fourteen thousand lighthouses bringing hope, direction, and light to the world.

PART ONE
THE MAN

CHAPTER 1

THE PATH

LOOKING FOR ASHWAY FARM

Everything was green. And everything was every shade of green. Moss, grass, fern, and leaf were woven together, blanketing the rolling hills of southwest England. Yellow hay bales and white sheep dotted the slopes. Narrow roads cut through in winding, shimmering ribbons, softened by hazy, low-hanging clouds.

My wife and I were driving a rental car down that ribbon of a road, taking in the sky, the damp air, and all that green.

We were thankful to have gotten out of London alive.

From my American perspective, I was driving on the wrong side of the car and on the wrong side of the road. I certainly had the wrong sense of direction. As I circled through roundabouts, going counterclockwise—the right way, right?—I had the opportunity to learn a few curse words courtesy of the local drivers.

Regardless, we were here, in an English countryside alive with beauty. We drove through tiny towns on cobblestone streets, passed stone pubs and quaint English houses.

But our hearts were longing to see the farm. I wanted to walk the paths where George Williams walked. I wanted to touch the ground and smell the earth. I wanted to pray as he had prayed, along the cart path that changed everything.

I love the YMCA. I have spent much of the past two decades learning and telling its story. I have helped to build many YMCAs in developing countries, have trained employees on several continents, and have spent countless hours in old, dusty books, unpacking this organization's rich history. I am privileged to witness YMCA heroes leading orphanages, feeding starving children, running halfway homes to rescue women from the streets, and mentoring young people all over the world. Continually I am stunned by the incredible reach of the YMCA, by the brilliance and power of its light.

But when I tell people the YMCA is one of the greatest mission organizations in the world, transforming lives in more than 120 countries, I usually get a confused response.

Most reply that those four letters merely bring to mind a family friendly health club or a song by the Village People.

When I talk about its founder—his heart, his passion, his resilience, his vision—most don't even recognize the name George Williams.

How could a mission movement unparalleled in history be mostly known as a "gym and swim"?

We drove through the Exmoor forest, and for a short time a wild pony galloped alongside us, much to my wife's delight. Then we headed southwest through the moorland to the tiny town of Dulverton, nestled in the county of Somerset.

Dulverton, as I said, is tiny. Its population is barely more than one thousand. Any other day, we could have spent the afternoon navigating the shops along cobblestone streets, chatting with the locals in an ancient pub, or exploring the church grounds up on the hill. This day we went to the library. There we tracked down a few maps that we hoped would help us find Ashway Farm—George Williams's childhood home.

The maps were not helpful. The roads were not roads. Maybe they were paths. Corn scraped both sides of our little rental car as we barreled along. We got lost. We kept driving. We got lost some more. We stopped the car to take a break and breathe some English air. Driving, and then lost again, we intersected a "road" and had to slam on the brakes to avoid hitting another car.

The car came to a stop, and a woman stepped out. In a rich accent she asked, "What are you looking for?" (We must have looked like confused Americans.)

Exhausted and eager for any kind of help, I said, "Well, could you point us to Ashway Farm?"

To my surprise, she said, "That would be our farm! Come now, follow me."

Nothing could have prepared us for the beauty of this English farm. We followed our newfound friend down the little road to a cheery yellow farmhouse. Across the yard was a barn and a pen filled with cottony, white sheep. The farm itself was set into rolling hills, circled by well-worn footpaths, and overflowing with hay. There was so much hay. The bales were enormous, and they rolled over the hills as far as the eye could see. Our new friends were hay farmers.

They couldn't have been kinder or more hospitable. We met their kids, toured the farm, walked the hills, and found the path that changed history.

Behind the farm there is a simple path that winds down the hillsides, through farmland, and toward the ever-increasing sound of rushing water. This path leads to the Tarr Steps—a medieval clapper bridge built of large, beautiful stones which crosses the River Barle in Exmoor National Park.

And just like my wife and I did those years ago on Ashway Farm, we, too, will come around to that path. I'm going to ask you to walk it with me.

But before we do, let's begin with a birthday.

BORN TO BE A FARMER

On October 11, 1821, Elizabeth Williams gave birth to her eighth and last child, a son, whom she named George. She might have hoped for a daughter—after all, she and her husband, Amos, already had seven boys! Nevertheless, another boy meant more help with the hay at Ashway Farm.

I come from a family of four boys and have four sons of my own. I know that there is something that comes with being the youngest, and can't imagine much has changed, even in the past two hundred years. The youngest

Williams would benefit from the protection of seven older brothers, but would be the recipient of a bit of brotherly harassment, too.

George took his place in the household, and his cheerful presence made him the life of the family. Sometimes his demeanor led to daydreams and big questions about life, and sometimes it manifested in anxiety (he was known to be "high-strung"). He would have to put all that aside to take up the role of a steadfast, grounded hay farmer in the tradition of the Williamses of Ashway Farm.[1]

THERE HAS TO BE MORE

For a while George was able to attend school in town, but each day when school ended, he returned to the farm to tackle chores. He led sheep in and out of pasture and was responsible for hauling hay carts up and down meandering paths. This was not a favorite chore. Generations of carts riding over the same dirt paths created deep ruts which were a challenge in dry weather and disastrous when it rained. George breathed a sigh of relief every day that the cart didn't get stuck—or worse, tip over.

George was a dreamer. So perhaps it was while he did the daily, monotonous, difficult work of hauling hay that he began to dream and wonder whether there might be more to life than what he saw in front of him every day and every year. This dreaming and wondering began to build into a deep, soul longing. "There has to be more."[2]

Many of us have felt what George did: a profound yearning to be part of a different story, to break the mold, to chart a new course.

EMPTY RELIGION

For all the dreaming and longing in young George's heart, Ashway Farm moved on at the same pace it always had. There were rhythms to the farm, and his life fell into line. Each weekday was full of farmwork and schoolwork, Saturday was more farmwork, and on Sunday the Williams family attended the Dulverton church.

Many of the greatest minds—creative, philosophical, scientific minds—have been inspired and captured by what they've learned in church. Exposure to a greater mind, a greater love, and great hope has done much to fill and excite the hungry soul.

Unfortunately, that was not the experience young George had in church. Church was a dull and empty practice, a time-consuming commitment to rule keeping and religious performance. Aside from the possibility of a quick nap and a few daydreams, the whole experience left him in a greater state of longing.

George's childhood church failed in its most essential mission—the exciting task of making the creator God known and inviting people to know Him. Nevertheless, this church did have one perk.

After each service, the parishioners would head outside for an afternoon of athleticism and competition.[3] There were wrestling matches, horseshoes, hoop rolling, and tag. Might this combination of faith and sports have laid the groundwork for the holistic vision of the YMCA?

George Williams was born to be a farmer; he was born into a tiny town; he attended a small church with a small view of God. His story of mundane work and dead religion seemed to have been written for him without his consent. A beloved twenty-first-century children's author ends a favorite book with this phrase: "If you ever find yourself in the wrong story, leave."[4] At a tender age George began to wonder if perhaps, just perhaps, he might have been meant for a different story.

A TIPPING POINT

It was a day like any other day. Young George was leading a hay cart along the Tarr Steps path, his mind lost in dreams and longings. He was still far from the house and barn when a crash of thunder startled him from his imaginations. The sky went black, save for flashes of lightning along the horizon. George hurried the cart along, hoping to beat the storm. Nothing would be worse than a muddy path and a cart full of sopping wet hay.

His worry and haste made him just a little careless. In the rush to get home, he lost control of the cart. A wheel caught in a rut, the cart spun out, and hay flew everywhere. George was thrown into a ditch, and as he lay there, covered in mud and stubble, the storm unleashed upon him.

He felt not unlike the overturned cart that lay on its side in the rain. Was he nothing more than a machine that traveled back and forth, back and forth, back and forth, along paths that others had forged? "There has to be more!"

———————————

When his parents and brothers saw the muddy mess of young George, they decided it was time for a family conversation. George was fun, energetic, and bright; he was farm tough and resilient. But that day everyone agreed that George Williams was not meant to be a hay farmer. With the family gathered round, George's father said, "It's time for you to leave the farm.

How about drapes?"

CHAPTER 2
ONWARD AND OUTWARD

I am a dad of four sons. I have watched boys become men and have observed the great tensions of early teenage years. There is an inner battle between insecurity and overconfidence, between heartache and joy. Boys of this age are discovering their skills, their interests, and perhaps even their purpose. They very much want to be men but have some years to go before they leave childhood behind. It was during this season that fifteen-year-old George said goodbye to the farm.

He and his father rode together over those rutted paths one last time. All of George's belongings were packed into the horse cart, and all his family and friends were left behind. I wonder what George was thinking as he bumped along the path toward Bridgwater in 1836. Did he feel like he had let his father down? Was he excited to find something more? Was he scared? Was he ready for adventure? He surely had no idea what life after Ashway Farm would look like.

While we may never have a full picture of the complexities of young George Williams, he tells us a little about himself in a reflection many years later: "I entered Bridgwater a careless, thoughtless, godless, swearing young fellow."[1]

MR. HOLMES'S FACTORY

George was exchanging farm life for factory life. He was to be trained as a draper. In the mid-nineteenth century, the term *draperies* did not refer merely to curtains, as it does now. Draperies referred to textiles in general, including fabrics, clothing, and home linens. George would join twenty-seven other young men who lived and worked in the factory building—a place owned and managed by a Mr. Holmes of Bridgwater.

Such factories were usually terrible working environments. Young people, including children, worked excessive hours with little rest. Illnesses associated with factory work were rampant, especially respiratory disease caused by inhaling fabric fibers. Children who worked in factories were often unnaturally pale, with distorted postures and crippled limbs; these resulted from hours working in one position inside dark, dreary, windowless rooms. It was not uncommon for factory workers to be missing fingers, even hands, because of unsafe machinery.[2] Childhood innocence was lost to violence, drunkenness, loneliness and lack of love. Factory workers were deplete of joy and desperate for hope.

Mr. Holmes's factory, however, seems to have been slightly different. This man genuinely cared for his working family and wanted to create a wholesome environment where young men could develop good character. To this end, Holmes insisted that his entire factory attend the old Zion Congregational Chapel on Sunday mornings. This was unusual. Most factory workers did not have time to attend Sunday services, and those who did often spent Sunday getting drunk instead. While George might have appreciated the day off and the kind nature of Mr. Holmes, he resented attending church. A "thoughtless, active, capable young man, with a hasty temper and a warm heart,"[3] George was much more interested in fun and friendship. He had had enough of empty religion and didn't want to be forced into a rigid system of beliefs and behavior.

Despite this, George seemed to thrive in his new world, at least initially. He was no stranger to long, hard days of work. The farm had made him resilient and tough. He worked efficiently and gained respect as a strong worker. On the surface it seemed George was adapting well. In the quietness of his heart, however, restless longing lingered.

Several months into his time at Holmes's factory, George noticed something about two of his fellow apprentices. These young men seemed to have a glow about their lives. They seemed at peace. They lived with purpose. They treated people with patience. They were joyful, even within the monotony of factory life. George found himself drawn to whatever it was that made them so different.[4]

Finally, he had to know the difference. He approached them and struck up a conversation. The young men invited George to visit their church on Sunday evening.

George uttered an unconvinced yes. Was this really going to be the answer? Church? Religion? He'd had his fill of lifeless sermons as a child, and now Sunday after Sunday he was forced to sit through services at the boss's church instead of enjoying what could have been precious free time. How could he possibly find at a new church what he was looking for? At the same time, there was something so intriguing and compelling about his young friends' lives that he decided he must see what they were experiencing.

FIRST LOVE

One winter evening not long afterward, sixteen-year-old George found himself seated with those friends in the back row of a tiny chapel on Frairn Street. He came with questions, longings, and just a little bit of hope. His heart was open and he listened intently. The minister was a man named Reverend Evan James. He was not a remarkable pastor or a famous author. He wasn't known to be powerful, eloquent, or influential. One of the only remaining descriptions of this pastor is that he was "a man of gentle spirit and holy life, whose grasp of principle was very firm."[5] No one remembers the exact sermon or the Bible passage from which he preached that evening, but when George heard it, something shifted in his heart. A light turned on, and he began to understand something that he had not before.

I have been a pastor for more than twenty years, and I have seen those lightbulb moments many times. They are one of the great delights of my life. Lights don't turn on when people sit in church and hear lists of rules and regulations. They don't flicker when we hear about what we need to do. But they blaze when we hear about what Christ has done. It is a joy to tell people God loves them more than they could ever comprehend, and He wants a relationship with them. Evan James would have taught, as I do, that though each of us are separated from God because of our sinful choices, Jesus lived a perfect life that we could never live. He died on a cross, taking the penalty of our sin and offering us His

27

forgiveness. He rose from the grave, victorious over sin and death. Through a relationship with Jesus, people can experience a new kind of life with God, full of strength, joy, and purpose. He made a way for any person to experience a deep, personal connection with God that can be theirs today and that will last forever in heaven. Jesus was and is the life that is the light of all humankind (John 1:4).

After the service, George's friends told him how he could have this new life. They encouraged him, "Confess your sins, accept Christ, trust in Him, yield your heart to the Savior."[6]

Something changed forever in the heart of George Williams that snowy evening. Back at the factory, he knelt on the floor and spoke to God. Later in his life, George described this moment. "God helped me," he said simply, "to yield myself wholly to Him. I cannot describe to you the joy and peace which flowed into my soul when first I saw that the Lord Jesus had died for my sins, and that they were all forgiven."[7]

This moment was the great turning point of George's life. He encountered God and began a relationship with Him that became the anchor of his heart and the driving purpose of his life. Though George's life was not perfect nor trouble free, he would never live it alone. A relationship with Jesus replaced empty religion. Joy and peace took the place of longing and searching. What he had seen in his friends' lives was now planted in his own heart.

Years later Williams said, "It is not easy to forget one's first love. I first learnt in Bridgwater to love my dear Lord and Savior for what He had done for me."[8]

I have visited the spot where that tiny chapel once stood. A small group of YMCA leaders from seven countries met in Bridgwater and stood together on the street outside. We thanked God that He is still transforming hearts everywhere. We marveled at the beautiful story that has stretched out from that unknown corner of the world.

Now, this is a beautiful story, but it is not made up of famous, powerful people. The stories of the YMCA are those of people like Evan James. Faithful men and women who have invested their lives in the people right in front of them. T-ball coaches and wellness instructors, front desk greeters, and childcare workers. All those faithful ones who serve on committees or help to clean up buildings. The YMCA story consists of people who care deeply for lonely, searching youth like George Williams and for each member of the YMCA community. The story is woven through with men and women who shine brightly with God's love for humanity.

TO LONDON

My second son is nineteen, and as I write this, it is not hard for me to imagine some of his adventurous spirit in nineteen-year-old George Williams. Nineteen—youthful freedom and responsible adulthood are crashing together; the whole world seems to be just around the next bend.

After George spent a few years at the Holmes drapery establishment, his apprenticeship ended. In 1841 he packed up from the bunkhouse and moved in with an older brother, Fred. Fred was newly married and setting up shop in a village near Bridgwater. He planned a several-day supply run in London and invited George to join him. They hoped that while they were there, Fred could introduce George to a Mr. Hitchcock of the Hitchcock and Rogers' Drapery establishment, and that George might gain employment in the city.

The introduction did not go well. Hitchcock took one look at George and said, "No! I've no place for him. He's too small!"[9] Fred might have responded with the 1800s version of a comeback: "It's not the size of the dog in the fight; it's the size of the fight in the dog!" In any case he assured

Mr. Hitchcock that while George was small, he was feisty and could do the work. Hitchcock, not completely persuaded, invited the duo back in the morning to hear his final word.

The next day George was as anxious as any young man headed to a second interview. But somehow in the night Mr. Hitchcock had softened a degree or two, and he agreed to give George a trial run.[10]

Soon afterward George was hired as a junior assistant for an annual salary of thirty-five pounds.[11] He was set to work as a draper in Hitchcock and Rogers with 140 other young men. This mass of men were at their stations working at seven o'clock in the morning and put down their tools at nine o'clock at night. Winter allowed a slight reprieve: they clocked out one hour earlier.[12] As stern as Mr. Hitchcock was, everyone knew that there were plenty of other young men at other factories working even longer hours.

Nighttime meant crowding, squeaking springs, snoring, and restless tossing, as even the smallest factory dorm room was crammed with two or three beds. Two men, strangers until they started work at the factory, slept together (or tried to sleep) in each bed.

"I SEE NO MEANS OF GRACE"

It was a strange sight. In the darkness, out of a high factory bunkhouse window, a Wellington boot lowered slowly toward the ground and then hovered three feet above the street. The door to the Goose and Gridiron, a gritty pub, squeaked open, and a barkeep stepped out. He filled the boot with bottles of booze and then gave a whistle. At this signal the boot began its slow journey back up to the window of the bunkhouse.[13] Crowd one hundred young men together in a dorm, and they're bound to find ways to have a good time.

No matter their stealthy attempts at fun, George, even at nineteen, saw the darkness and desperation that had settled upon his friends on the factory floor.

The very first Young Men's Christian Association Report, written in 1844, reflects on these times.

> Until recently the young men engaged in the pursuits
> of business were totally neglected. They were treated
> as though deprived of mind, as though formed only
> to labor and sleep, and to sleep and labor, so that they
> could only go from their beds to the counter, and
> from the counter to their beds, without a moment for
> mental or spiritual culture, without the disposition
> or even the strength for the performance of those

devotional exercises which are necessary for the maintenance of a spiritual life.[14]

One hundred and fifty thousand men had come to London in a matter of years, seeking work, seeking significance, longing for something more. Was this it? Sixteen-hour days, tiny rooms shared with strangers, little time to eat or sleep. Wonderings and daydreams were dimming like so many flickering candles.

George Williams, looking around at that factory floor, at his friends, his fellow workers, his generation, said, "I [see] no means of grace."[15] What he did see was emptiness, aimlessness, hurt, and struggle. He felt he was watching the bright hopefulness of youth fade away. He stood watching, and he didn't know what to do.

One of the greatest global movements that the world has ever seen began because a kid did not know what to do. So he did the only thing he could do. He began to pray. He began to pray name by name for his fellow employees.[16] Yes, it was a dark time. But light shines brightest in the darkness.

THE POWER OF PRAYER

As George was on his knees on the floor of dorm room 14, "the loneliness, temptation, and irreligion of his surroundings led him to pour out his heart in prayer that he might find a fellow-worker among the young men."[17] It seems a small thing, but I think it is powerful that George recognized his need for a friend and a partner. I still occasionally need to be reminded that my light shines brighter when I am linked with brothers and sisters. This kid was a teenager, yet he understood that "he" was not nearly as strong as "we."

Less than a month later, a twenty-four-year-old man named Christopher Smith was hired at Hitchcock and Rogers and moved into Williams's dorm. Smith was a genuine follower of Jesus and, like George, wanted to use his time and influence to love and serve others.[18] Now there were two young men praying at Hitchcock and Rogers.

They began to pray together for their fellow laborers at the factory. They prayed for Mr. Hitchcock and Mr. Rogers too. These friends must have prayed on the factory floor, used their precious "free time" to pray, and cut into their sleep to pray. They must have squeezed in among other roommates, the beds, and the trunks to pray. This was not rule following or dead religion: this was the hope, certainty, and love that they each had found, shining out of their lives.

The other men must have noticed. Perhaps word got around that some "religious" kids were in room 14. However it happened, others came to the door, knocked, and were invited in. George, Christopher, and the others encouraged each other after long, hard days. They studied the Bible together, strengthening and shaping their understanding of a loving and gracious God. As they prayed, their little group began to grow.

An early biographer of George Williams said that when Williams came to Hitchcock and Rogers, "it was almost impossible for a young man in the house to be a Christian," but three years later "it was almost impossible to be anything else."[19]

The company was transformed. Eventually all the employees, plus Mr. Hitchcock and Mr. Rogers, had joined weekly prayer meetings and Bible studies.

Men in darkness were drawn to the light and life they saw in George and his new brothers. When they heard about the real Jesus, they wanted to know more. A revolution of kindness, hope, and love was building inside Hitchcock and Rogers. Significance was replacing aimlessness. Light was shining in the darkness.

OUT OF THE FACTORY

One hundred and fifty thousand men had come to work in the darkness of London factories, and it did not sit well with George that light shone for so few. Ever a man of longing, George began to wonder whether it would be possible to grow their little movement out of the walls of Hitchcock and Rogers and into greater London. "That was the question that throbbed within the heart of George Williams. 'If,' said he,

'God has so blessed us in this house, why should he not give such a blessing in every house of London?'"[20]

With these thoughts and questions buzzing around in his mind, George met up with his good friend Edward Beaumont, or Teddy, as he called him. As they walked from St. Paul's Cathedral, across Blackfriars Bridge, and toward Surrey Chapel, George shared his burden. Sometimes it takes a walk with a friend to bring a vision out of one's mind and into reality.

Blackfriars Bridge with St. Paul's Cathedral in the background, London, 1880's [21]

Teddy remembered it like this: "After walking a few

minutes in silence you said, pressing my arm and addressing me familiarly, as you were in the habit of doing, 'Teddy, are you prepared to make a sacrifice for Christ?' I replied, 'If called upon to do so, I hope and trust I can.' You then told me that you had been deeply impressed with the importance of introducing religious services, such as we enjoyed, into every large establishment in London, and that you thought that if a few earnest, devoted, and self-denying men could be found to unite themselves together for this purpose, that with earnest prayer God would smile upon their efforts, and much good might be done."[22]

George and Teddy weren't the only ones who wanted to see the light grow in London. Mr. Hitchcock himself, newly a follower of Christ, eagerly described the gatherings taking place in his dorms to proprietors of other local factories. He was excited about the change he saw in his young men and thought everyone else should know what was happening. Soon no fewer than four drapery establishments were hosting prayer meetings for young men.[23]

Just days after George and Teddy walked Blackfriars Bridge, George received a post from James Smith, the principal assistant at a nearby dry goods enterprise. He wrote, "I have been truly rejoiced to hear that the Lord is doing a great work in your house.... I am engaged here in the same work, but stand almost alone, and from what I have heard, I am induced to say, 'Come over and help us.'"[24]

Something bigger than any one man was glowing and growing out of the gritty, dirty, lonely factories of industrial London. One precious person at a time was being transformed, was being made alive, was being fueled by the love he had received, and was becoming eager to spread the flame.

THE YOUNG MEN'S CHRISTIAN ASSOCIATION

In the same week that George received that post saying, "Come over and help us," he, Christopher Smith, James Smith, and nine other men made plans to meet once again in room 14. Aside from James Smith, everyone in the room was a laborer at Hitchcock and Rogers. Well over half were men whom George and Christopher had prayed for by name and who had come to know Christ at the factory. These were the men Williams loved.

> *George Williams was one of the first to realize that there is a distinct class, a great race of workers ... whose need is as deep as any in London. These men of the middle class, of shop and warehouse, of stool and counter, make no loud appeal for help.... [They] suffer silently and in loneliness, for such is the way of "respectability."*
>
> *But George Williams was one of them, one with them. And he knew.*[25]

These factory men whom Williams knew, loved, and prayed for crowded into room 14 one more time. By all accounts it was an informal meeting. Hearts were burdened, light was shining, they were moving toward a tipping point; even so, none of the twelve could know the significance of their little gathering.

Williams didn't document the occasion at all. Instead his diaries from that period show that he was amid a struggle. He was wrestling with God over his own heart. He confessed ingratitude, unbelief, and a judgmental spirit.[26]

Twelve factory laborers—poor, undereducated, and so recently lost in nameless, faceless crowds; a leader humbly struggling with his own weaknesses; a tiny factory dorm room. Together in this upper room, these young men sought the Lord, and He answered.

Their power was in their weakness. Williams's lifestyle of prayer is a picture of that dynamic: he would be the asker, and God would be the giver. It was their great need, rather than their great qualifications, that allowed God's power, wisdom, and love to flow freely.

They met that day to pray, and they left with the seed of a movement that would transform lives around the world. Christopher Smith suggested that they call it the Young Men's Christian Association—the YMCA.[27]

In his journal Edward Valentine summarized what happened in room 14 that day: "Thursday, June 6, 1844. Met in George Williams' room for the purpose of forming a society, the object of which is to influence religious young men to spread the Redeemer's Kingdom amongst those by whom they're surrounded."[28]

Across from the King David Hotel in the Old City of Jerusalem stands one of the most beautiful buildings I have seen: the Jerusalem International YMCA. The letters *YMCA* signal both hope and welcome to the entire city from their place on its Tower. This YMCA has stood for almost one hundred years as a symbol of light, life, and health. While most travelers who stop to climb the tower or to admire the architecture will never know this, inside there is an exact replica of George Williams's room 14.

I was able to visit with some other YMCA leaders in 2020. There, in that upper room, several of us huddled together in prayer. In a moment tethering us to twelve men who had lived two centuries earlier, we prayed that the same burning light that glowed in them would be alive in our hearts.

ONWARD

In late July, one month after George and his friends launched the fledgling Young Men's Christian Association, the twelve drafted a letter, hoping to circulate it to an ever-widening group of London factory workers. The newly formed YMCA, however, had no funds, and of course the letters wouldn't be delivered for free. Some suggested dropping the campaign, setting aside the invitation until they were funded. George Williams, ever the confident leader, slammed his fist on the table and exclaimed, "If this is of God, the money will come!"[29] Williams wasn't blurting out some throwaway phrase. He saw himself as a player in a spiritual work more powerful than his capacities, larger than his moment in history, and supplied by the very generosity, grace, and love of God. Williams led and worked in a way both constrained and energized by that power.

And yes, the money came.

Already the little group had outgrown the tiny upper room and were renting a local coffee shop for meetings: St. Martins at Ludgate Hill. When seventy men responded to the invitations, they outgrew the coffee shop. They crossed the street and rented Radley's Hotel and Pub. Not long afterward they outgrew the pub and moved to Sergeant's Inn, a space big enough for hundreds of young men from all over the city. The vision that came into focus on Blackfriars Bridge was taking form. The light was spreading.

Looking back, we see the directionality of this time: onward and outward. This spiritual outpouring that began with one man grew in size and momentum until it spilled out of London and spread around the world, transforming, reconciling, and empowering men and women who themselves became agents of love and change.

George Williams, founder of the YMCA[29]

CHAPTER 3
FINISHING WELL

A FAITHFUL LIFE

George Williams, the nineteen-year-old, started a movement in a factory dorm room which has stretched the globe and today impacts hundreds of thousands of lives. His longings, his love for others, and his confidence in Christ motivated this movement and the rest of his life.

George fell in love and married Helen Hitchcock when he was thirty-two. (Yes, Helen was the daughter of *that* Mr. Hitchcock—the owner of Hitchcock and Rogers.) After taking over the business from Mr. Hitchcock, George and Helen went on to have five children, all boys except for their youngest, Nellie, who died tragically when she was nineteen.[2] Helen was a true life partner, who "devoted herself day and night through more than fifty years to her husband and to the work they both loved."[3]

Despite a full and significant life, Williams avoided the spotlight. Even when, as an old man, he received a letter from the prime minister of England, extending a commendation to knighthood by the queen herself, Williams's first instinct was to refuse. J. H. Putterill, the general secretary of the London YMCA, was with him when the letter arrived, and later recalled his words to Williams: "Well sir, I knew you would refuse if you saw it for yourself alone—but see it for the YMCA—as an honor for them."[4] Williams thanked him for this new perspective and made two requests: that he be left alone to pray about the matter, and that Mrs. Williams not be told of the queen's invitation.[5] He was knighted in 1894, eleven years before his death.

Those later years were, in many ways, remarkably like the years spent in the dorms of Hitchcock and Rogers: steadfast, humble, faithful, energized by his faith. Williams's successes didn't alter his path. He didn't spin off countless projects. He was content to live a life consistent with the truth and love he first tasted as a young man.

He remained attentive to the details of his work, passionate that a good Christian must be a good business-man. As, one by one, YMCAs were planted around the globe, Williams traveled to visit, speak, and encourage. Other leaders occasionally called him in to help resolve frustrating issues in their chapters. His financial stability allowed him to make generous donations to less fortunate YMCAs. He regularly taught Sunday school at his home church.

No epic stories emerged from the quiet life of George Williams, yet he made an impression on the lives of all the people he touched. Perhaps the best way to describe the decades of his life is simply to point to the values of his life, which have become significant values in the YMCA.

VALUES OF THE MAN AND HIS MISSION

CARING

Williams was asked to speak about how a YMCA could grow and be successful. He could have said so many things! He could have talked about organization, delegation, advertising, or funding. But instead he said this:

> Get to know the names of young men. Take one at a time. Write a letter to him. Give him a shake of the hand. Ask him to have a friendly cup of tea. Talk kindly, naturally, with him. Take him for a walk. Show him a little kindness and you will get hold of him.... Have warm hearts, loving, big souls. By God's blessing there will be no failure. By using these means every difficulty will be surmounted.[6]

Above all, George Williams cared for people. He cared, even in the face of criticism, disagreement, and open hostility.

Williams told the story of a young man from the days at Hitchcock and Rogers who made it his goal to antagonize the few young men who were meeting to pray in room 14. If a person was known to have put his faith in Christ, this man would push back, making a point to tell him that his newfound beliefs were all nonsense and that he could easily talk him out of it. "Naturally," Williams said, "he was at once marked out ... for special and particular prayer."[7]

This young man only became increasingly combative. Williams continued to pray, and in addition he began to ask around the factory to find out about this man—specifically, what kinds of things he liked. A mutual friend knew that this guy could not pass up a good oyster dinner. So George and the room 14 men organized a night out for oysters and invited him along.

"The idea of these Christian young men indulging in such frivolity amused him immensely, and in a spirit of bravado he accepted their invitation."[8] When the night was over, it was not amusement or bravado that moved him but appreciation for the friendliness, care, and genuine kindness of George Williams and his companions.

It wasn't long before this man changed his mind and trusted in Christ too. George and his friends cared, but it wasn't a transactional affection; it was sourced in and motivated by the same care poured out on them by Jesus.

RESPECT

The Y in YMCA stands for "young," and while of course the YMCA is not only for the young, it is important that it was dreamed up by a young person, brought to life by young people, and served young people.

While young people are often undervalued and over-looked in favor of those who carry capital, experience, and influence, Williams not only saw the needs but respected the potential of the hundreds of thousands of young men in his city.

> *George Williams ... had the magic faculty of convincing every young man present that upon him rested the vast responsibility of making the meeting, and even the Association, a success. And when you have filled a young man with the belief that so much depends upon his strength and faithfulness, you have gone a good way towards making him a hero.*[9]

Under Williams, the YMCA pioneered a youth movement which is now characteristic of Christian ministry around the world. Simply, he recognized and respected the distinct value of young people.[10]

HONESTY

Of course, George Williams is best known as the founder of the YMCA. He was also, all his life, a businessman. Stacking the books or inflating a claim could have been a regular temptation. George wasn't above such temptation; rather he knew he had to be on guard against it. In his diary he wrote out a prayer, asking the Lord to keep him from "colouring and exaggeration." He went on: "Strengthen my memory, and bless me in all I do. May I in business act as though Mr. Hitchcock were standing by. Oh, my Father, help me to be conscientious in all I do.... Guide my judgement and keep me in the right way."[11]

This kind of radical honesty is one of the things that endears George Williams to me most. He humbly presented himself as he was, to people and to God. Honesty is, after all, about so much more than not telling a lie. It is about presenting truth, no matter the cost. George was convinced that his security and value were based not on his own performance but on his status as a loved son of God. Because of this, he was able to tell the truth about his own weaknesses and live life freely and honestly.

RESPONSIBILITY

George Williams was friendly, gregarious, big-hearted, and a dreamer. These qualities aren't always paired with things like organization, follow-through, and discipline.

It's interesting, then, but not surprising, that of the few papers found in his desk when he died, one is a set of goals for daily life. It was creased and worn, having been carried and read regularly. Let me share a few of these goals with you. I think you'll see how earnest Williams was about living a responsible life.

> The Lord be pleased to help me form resolutions and then give me grace to keep them.
>
> That I determine to get an alarm and when it goes off that I am out of bed before it is finished.
>
> That I read and meditate upon a portion of God's Word every morning and spend some time in prayer.
>
> That I spend some more time in praying for the young men at St. Paul's.
>
> That I have certain days and times for certain things and strive to be regular and punctual.
>
> That I strive to gain a better knowledge of the Scriptures and have Bible readings with dear Helen.[12]

Because of his humble nature, Williams, even to the end of his life, wanted to become more responsible, and he asked the Lord for grace to do that.

All of this is well and good. It is important to wake up on time and to have some discipline for the important things in life. We call this being responsible. Williams was, however, consistently responsible in a different way that made a significant impact.

He never saw a problem as someone else's problem.

One coworker from the factory floor remembered that "when anyone was behindhand and hard pressed with work, George Williams was always the first to assist, and gave his aid ungrudgingly and with the utmost cheeriness. He was never too busy, too weary, to be of service, and if ever a man were in a scrape, it was to George Williams that he appealed."[13]

Of course, this is just one snapshot of a lifestyle of responsibility: George did not sit on the sidelines. His whole life was shaped by the concern he felt and the responsibility he took for the world around him.

INCLUSION

George Williams related to people based on their inherent dignity, regardless of their age, ethnicity, socioeconomic status, or religious background. He called the YMCA to pray for and to regard "every young man in the kingdom." *Regard* means to consider and to see. So often, in our busy lives, we do not in fact see others. We don't look at them. This can be especially true when those others are somewhere outside our insular bubble.

Williams saw people. He included people. He wove regard and respect for every person into the fabric of the YMCA. "Every young man in the kingdom, from the Prince of Wales down to the lowest beggar, every young man from fourteen to forty"[14] was to be seen as a valuable person. In this light, he contended for unity and opened his arms wide for all.

Long ago Williams led the YMCA in this way, and to say that today we are grateful is an understatement.

HOLISTIC

The Young Men's Christian Association was born out of a conviction that the pivotal need of each person is a right relationship with their Creator. If this relationship is broken, then everything else is too; if it is reconciled, then a foundation is laid for flourishing.

Very early in the evolution of the YMCA, it became apparent that a significant implication of this right relationship would be holistic restoration and strengthening. Christian work is spiritual work, and as such it is human work; humans are spiritual beings. One early YMCA historian says that, yes, Christian ministries "do lead men to become Christians, [and] serving Jesus Christ does lead Christians to provide for the needs of the whole man."[15]

Dr. Luther Gulick, at the 1889 YMCA Convention, said, "The Associations have a very valuable foundation for their work in the fact that they are working for young men, not simply for their bodies, minds, and souls, but for the salvation, development, and training of the whole man complete, as God made him."[16]

To this day, the YMCA delights in viewing its members as whole persons, valuable and capable of flourishing in every way.

THE LIGHT SHINES ON

Not everyone finishes well. A certain complacency and self-satisfaction creeps in as we age, which quickly turns into small-mindedness, a desire to control, and fear of the unknown.

We don't see that in the life of George Williams.

At his last public address, Williams was frail, unable to stand or even read his prepared speech. Nevertheless, he was himself. He was the man God had been shaping ever since his days at Ashway Farm. He was humble, joyful, loving, passionate, and convinced.

A friend read his words to the crowd.

> *Go forward. Expect great things from God. Next to the peace and joy which have come to me through my Lord and Savior Jesus Christ, my greatest happiness has been found in the work of the Association. I would, therefore, urge upon all young men to give themselves, body, soul, and spirit, to the Savior who loved them and died for them, and to spend their lives in seeking to extend His kingdom. Thus shall come to them satisfaction and peace in this world and eternal glory in the life to come.*[17]

Can you see it? Can you see that bright, radiant flame burning in the heart of George Williams, even into his last days? I do. I see that same light shining in my own Countryside YMCA, and in YMCAs across the world. I am so grateful that this one man—this teenager—shared the light he had with those around him. And people have passed on that light, one after the other, for two hundred years.

—————————————

If you are ever in London, take a tour of St. Paul's Cathedral. It is magnificent and awe-inspiring, an architectural wonder admired by many. There you can visit George Williams's final resting place. Swing by Westminster Abby and see the famous stained glass window that commemorates Sir George and the YMCA. Go to the original location of the drape factory which launched the YMCA movement. Stroll across Blackfriars Bridge. If possible, take a friend and pray for fresh vision. But above all, walk to a simple, easily over-looked pillar in the shadow of St. Paul's, near the statue of Saint Anne. Read the words inscribed on it. And whisper a prayer that you would see people the way George Williams saw people, and love people the way George Williams loved people. Pray that the love of God, which burned bright in George Williams, would burn in you!

The plaque on the pillar near St. Paul's Cathedral[18]

In the summer of 2017, twelve global leaders of the YMCA gathered around that pillar. It felt like a sacred moment. We took Communion, an ancient symbol of remembrance and hope. We were there to reflect and remember, and as we did, deep hope rose inside us.

In that circle we prayed. We prayed God would rekindle the fire that ignited the YMCA movement. We prayed we would share the same vision and zeal that the founders shared among themselves.

In that circle, and in our prayer, we were emboldened. We believe the YMCA will once again fulfill its great mission of being fourteen thousand lighthouses shining brightly within the communities of the world. And we believe we will see that vision fulfilled in our lifetime.

PART TWO
THE MISSION

THE PARIS BASIS

The Young Men's Christian Associations seek to unite those young men who, regarding Jesus Christ as their God and Savior, according to the Holy Scriptures, desire to be his disciples in their faith and in their life, and to associate their efforts for the extension of his Kingdom amongst young men.

Any differences of opinion on other subjects, however important in themselves, shall not interfere with the harmonious relations of the constituent members and associates of the World Alliance.

—the global mission statement of the YMCA[1]

CHAPTER 4
THE AIM

MISSION

Matt Emmons was going to win the gold medal. It was the 2004 Olympics in Athens, Greece. Emmons, a sharpshooter, was favored to win the 50-meter three-position rifle event. After nine spectacular shots, Matt was so far in the lead that he did not even need a bull's-eye to win. All he needed to fire was an 8.0, and he would win the gold. So Matt took aim. He fired. He scored an 8.1. But he lost the gold medal.

In what was called an "extremely rare mistake in an elite competition,"[55] Emmons fired a winning shot at the wrong target. His aim moved from the target in lane 2 to the target in lane 3, and a good shot fired at the wrong target received a score of zero.

He lost the gold because his aim had drifted.

Experienced leaders have drafted brilliant resources on mission, vision, and values. Organizations and individuals spend significant time shaping direction and goals. Most people, in business and in life, recognize how important it is to know where they are headed and how they will get there.

Mission conversation generally centers around energy and aim. An organization's energy (its passion and effort) must be focused, concentrated, and then launched precisely (its aim). Together, energy and aim lead to mission success: a good shot fired at the right target.

Without a clear target and a steady aim, however, it is impossible to fulfill a mission. Perhaps this is why we see relatively few organizations succeed: standing the test of time, remaining truly effective in terms of their goals. What is it about the YMCA that has allowed it to exist, expand, and effect change for close to two centuries? Could it be something particular about its aim, its mission?

We're about to dig deeply into the original mission and vision statements that stretch back to the days of George Williams. We'll see the formative heartbeat and passion on which the YMCA was built. We'll discover George Williams's target.

PERSONAL PASSION

I am passionate about the mission of the YMCA.

First of all, the themes of this mission have changed my life. My own story has had seasons of emptiness and searching, and like so many others in the history of the YMCA, I have found the same hope that George Williams found.

Deep in my heart, I believe this mission can be part of changing the world. From orphanages to rehabilitation programs, from homeless shelters to T-ball teams, I've seen the mission thrive all over the globe.

At the same time, my heart aches that our mission is so often unknown or misunderstood. We are *more* than a song by the Village People. We are *more* than a family friendly gym and swim.

As we look at the heart of the mission and at those who have lived the mission, we will encounter words like faith, the Bible, and transformation. We will read of men and women who are passionate, strong, and unwavering. The mission statements of the YMCA are in fact strong and bold. The first time I read these statements, I was taken aback by the strength of their conviction and the boldness of their claims. Maybe you were too.

I remember a conversation with the CEO of a large YMCA in America. After admitting that she was relatively unaware of her organization's mission, she acknowledged, "If we were to take our mission seriously, we would act like a Christian mission organization!"

In the face of such a distinct mission, we might find ourselves inclined to head down one of two paths. Both drift away from the goal.

One path is that for fear of offense, we might dilute and soften the language of the mission or even rewrite history. This erodes historical integrity. Many YMCAs around the world list honesty as a core value. With that in mind, let's consider the actual mission words which were written nearly two centuries ago and have been repeated and built upon ever since. As you will see, there is a reason why these words have stood strong and been reaffirmed through generations.

The other path is one of needless offense. It's no secret that in the name of Christ and His church, people have felt judged and rejected. Some of you may feel stung by this "religion gone bad." I am grieved by this. The heart of God is grieved by this as well.

A THIRD PATH

Perhaps there is a third path. I believe that the best way to approach the bold mission of the YMCA is to take the approach Jesus took. He once gave an extended teaching called the Sermon on the Mount. It has been called the greatest sermon ever preached by the greatest preacher who ever lived and is a message with much to say about living "on mission" in this world.

Jesus gives us two metaphors that are full of profound implications for this third path.

First, He says to His followers, "You are the salt of the earth" (Matt. 5:13 NIV).

In Jesus' time ancient Middle Eastern people had no way to keep perishable food cold. Left alone, meat immediately began to decay, and before long it would go bad. Salt preserves meat. Jesus' point is that his followers could live in such a way that they could help to preserve God's good plan in a decaying world. As the YMCA lives its bold mission, goodness and wholesomeness will be preserved in a world that is falling apart.

Salt not only preserves; it adds flavor. The Message version of the Bible translates Matthew 5:13 like this: "Let me tell you why you are here. You're here to be salt-seasoning that brings out the God-flavors of this earth. If you lose your saltiness, how will people taste godliness?"

When the historic mission statements of the YMCA are truly lived out, the God-flavors of joy, patience, hope, respect, and so many more are experienced in our YMCAs. When people take swim lessons and taste God's love, the

YMCA is living on mission. When kids go to a YMCA camp and taste hope, the YMCA is living on mission.

Jesus adds a second metaphor. He says, "Here's another way to put it: You're here to be light, bringing out the God-colors in the world. God is not a secret to be kept. We're going public with this, as public as a city on a hill. If I make you light-bearers, you don't think I'm going to hide you under a bucket, do you? I'm putting you on a light stand. Now that I've put you there on a hilltop, on a light stand—shine!" (Matt. 5:14–15 MSG).

Jesus says that living on mission should never be like keeping a light hidden under a bucket; we should shine out like light beaming from the hilltops.

AGAIN, THE LIGHTHOUSE

This reminds me of the picture I introduced at the beginning of this book. The YMCA is a lighthouse. Its mission is to shine. At YMCAs all over the world, you can find people shining by putting Christian principles like love, kindness, hope, and grace into practice in their communities.

The Bible says that "in [Jesus] was life, and that life was the light of all mankind. The light shines in the darkness, and the darkness has not overcome it" (John 1:4–5 NIV). There was something about the way Jesus lived, something about the way He loved, something about the way He led and interacted with people that was light shining in the darkness. This passage goes on to say that though the darkness was great, it was not greater than the light.

This is a time, a moment in our world, when things seem dark. People are anxious, are hurting, have lost jobs and buried loved ones. Many are wondering, "What's next?" and are searching for hope.

I believe that today can be the YMCA's finest moment. The original vision of the YMCA was that it would shine as a beacon, glowing with the Christian principles of hope, joy, love, and grace in the midst of darkness. People need help when a storm is raging. They're looking for direction and solid ground. The YMCA is more than a song, gym, or building. We are a lighthouse.

As we explore the mission of the YMCA, my hope and prayer is that we can follow Jesus' path of being salt and light.

"THE OLD THAT IS STRONG"

J. R. R. Tolkien wrote fantasies about hobbits, orcs, and magical rings. But in his stories we encounter much more than mythical creatures. Woven through are truths that seem to have prophetic depth.

A poem from Tolkien's *Lord of the Rings* hangs in my office. I often read it, and when I do, I can't help but think of the mission of the YMCA.

All that is gold does not glitter

   Not all those who wander are lost;

The old that is strong does not wither,

   Deep roots are not reached by the frost.

From the ashes a fire shall be woken,

   A light from the shadows shall spring;

Renewed shall be blade that was broken,

   The crownless again shall be king.[2]

Would you join me as we explore "the old that is strong"? There we will see the deeply rooted mission of the YMCA. We will stir the ashes a bit, and I believe that as we do, from the shadows we will see light!

CHAPTER 5

BEGINNINGS

THE MISSION EMERGES

As I mentioned earlier, the mission of the YMCA was not drafted in a board room strategy session. It began with a group of friends who felt the love of God could heal the brokenness around them. In the mid-nineteenth century, George Williams joined thousands of young men who made their way from rural, community-oriented villages to over-crowded cities. The grind of newly industrialized England was stifling their spirits, minds, and bodies.

It was in this haze, this machine, this emptiness and longing, that a vision began to build in Williams's heart and mind. He experienced a calling of sorts—a call to mission: to turn on the lights for those stumbling around in darkness.

George and a small group of like-minded friends—dirty, poor, and exhausted yet joyful and energized with love —began to coalesce around a vision. A journal entry from June 6, 1844, written by one of these young men, says that the purpose of the group was "to influence young men to spread the Redeemer's Kingdom amongst those by whom they are surrounded."[1]

I love the sentiment of this phrase, but it can be easy to get lost in the language. Let's take a minute to dig into a few of the significant words.

- *Redeemer* refers to "one who brings freedom." George and his friends saw oppression in their world and believed they had found a liberator.

- We don't use the term *kingdom* much these days, but Jesus used it all the time. The kingdom of God is a realm, both now and eternally, where God's kindness, justice, and love are poured out and where His creation flourishes as intended.

Williams and his friends at the factory wanted to announce the good news of the kingdom of love to everyday, unnoticed men: cogs in the machine of the kingdom of commerce. In the Redeemer's kingdom—the kingdom of love—these men were unique, valuable, significant, and free. Just as George had found significance, hope, grace, and love, he was passionate that other young men would too.

As George and his fellow change agents met together, they began to hone and clarify their mission, and soon they documented that their purpose was "improvement of the spiritual condition of the young men engaged in houses of business, by the formation of Bible classes, family and social prayer meetings, mutual improvement societies, or any other spiritual agency."[2]

It is unique and significant that Williams's original purpose was so focused on spiritual condition. Certainly, there was a whole array of conditions with which he might have been concerned. And surely he was. But Williams and his friends saw the spiritual landscape of the human heart as the primary space where meaningful change could occur.

And meaningful change did indeed occur. Within a year, with this mission as the foundation, eighteen more groups of young men were organized in the city of London. This means that in that year, scores of young men found what was missing in their lives, stepped out from the shadows, and stepped into the light of significance, hope, and community.

THE MISSION CROSSES THE SEA

Captain Thomas Sullivan lived an adventurous life. He whaled in the Antarctic, was shipwrecked there, sailed to Brazil, was attacked by pirates, and made and lost a fortune by the time he was thirty. When he was an older man, his adventures continued. He settled in Boston and there longed to create a home away from home for the lonely and rough-around-the-edges seamen who streamed through the harbor each day. Sullivan met those men at the docks, welcoming them home and seeing them off, and as he did, he shared the hope and love of Jesus Christ.[3]

About this time, Sullivan happened to read an article in a newspaper that described the growing YMCA movement in London. He wrote in a journal entry, "I read ... of this new organization in London that had been formed for young men who had pledged their lives to Jesus Christ and needed a wholesome alternative to life on the street. I thought this would fit my young men just fine."[4] Sullivan was a man of action, and without hesitation he got on a ship to London to visit the YMCA organization there. This was in October of 1851. By December he had returned, gathered a group of willing Christian leaders, and launched the first YMCA in America, at Old South Church in Boston.[5]

He addressed the public with a statement of purpose as he proclaimed that the association would become "a social organization of those in whom the love of Christ has produced love to men; who shall meet the young stranger as he enters our city, take him by the hand, direct him to a boarding house where he may find a quiet home pervaded with Christian influences ... and in every way throw around him good influences, so that he may feel he is not a stranger, but that noble and Christian spirits care for his soul."[6]

Thomas Sullivan too was motivated by a deep concern for the young men of his day. He had lived a rough-and-tumble life but evidently had found great hope and purpose in sharing the love and person of Jesus with others. It was out of this love—"the love of Christ [which] has produced love to men"[7]—that the mission of the YMCA in America began to unfold.

ONE GREAT AIM

Having launched the YMCA, George Williams was frequently asked if he would lend his energy and the name of the Y to other social efforts. Williams would decline, replying that "he had but one work, one great aim." He was a man of singular purpose. To Williams the "grandest work in the world"[8] was shining the light of Jesus. He believed that if people could know and trust Christ, they would have ever-growing hope, strength, and purpose. He would not be pulled off course.

There were many good social efforts in Williams's day, as there are in ours. I don't dispute the value of the many good works we see around the world! I merely wish to demonstrate that George Williams's mission, aim, and vision for the YMCA was that it would be based on his belief in the transforming power of Jesus.

REFLECTING ON THE MISSION

Many years after the YMCA was formed, Williams's good friend John Mott interviewed him about the original aim of the movement. Mott, winner of the Nobel Peace Prize and president of the World Alliance of YMCAs, had a deep understanding of its mission and purpose yet saw value in coming back to the foundation laid by its founder.

In the interview Mott asked, "What was in your mind and in the minds of your colleagues which led you to form the first Young Men's Christian Association?"

The answer to this question still shapes our movement today. The answer to this question points us toward the original target. I encourage you to read through Williams's response slowly and with great consideration.

Contemplating Mott's question, Williams thought for a moment, and with conviction replied, "We had only one thing in mind, and that was to bind our little company together in order that we might the better lead our comrades to Christ, and in order that we might share with one another our personal experience of Christ."[9]

Williams had only one thing in mind. He had a singular purpose: to build a community which would point to Christ. Jesus Christ had made all the difference in Williams's life: the light in the darkness, the source of hope, the source of love. Williams's decision to trust Christ was his North Star, and he overflowed with desire to build community around the love, life, and hope found in Jesus.

———————————

John R. Mott was the president of the World Alliance of YMCAs for twenty-one years. Shortly before he died, he gave his last message to the movement. Reflecting on the season that lay behind, he said,

> [It] has been one of pioneering, of pathfinding, and of adventure. It has been a period of entering doors opened by God. It has been a period of secure foundation laying; the foundations which have been laid have been broad, deep, solid, and capable of sustaining a great superstructure. It has been a century of seed sowing and watering, at times with tears, also of diligent cultivation, and as a result on all continents there have been ripened fields and marvellous harvests.[10]

Mott understood the importance of a strong foundation.

CHAPTER 6

FOUNDATIONS

BUILD ON SOMETHING SOLID

As I write this book in advance of George Williams's two hundredth birthday, my personal life has been exceptionally full. Along with writing, pastoring a church in a YMCA, and parenting our four boys, I'm also building a home. My wife and I had the creative vision (or crazy idea) to move an old farmhouse to a new piece of property and construct our home from the materials.

As a pastor, I tend to think in analogies. And yes, I've used the analogy of a firm foundation many times. But believe me, this concept has never been more real.

Every masonry and construction contractor emphasizes the importance of a solid foundation, which performs three basic functions.

1. *A firm foundation bears the load of the house.* This includes both the materials of the house and all of the people who will one day make the house their home. Without a strong foundation to bear the load, a house

will sink unevenly into the ground, weakening and cracking the structure.

2. *A firm foundation anchors the house against unpredictable external forces.* When the force of nature comes against a building, if the building has a firm foundation, the energy of wind and storms and floods will be channeled into the ground. Foundations are dug into the earth and are set in stone or concrete. A structure built on such a strong base can take a beating in a way that a structure merely set on top of the ground cannot.

3. *A firm foundation creates a barrier between the slow creep of ground moisture and the house.* While "the slow creep of ground moisture" doesn't sound too dramatic or dangerous, it will ruin a structure over time if not abated. (Think rot, mold, and accelerated deterioration.)

Foundations are never an afterthought. They are carefully planned and carefully constructed. While not the most exciting part of our new house, the foundation is assuredly the most important.

A FOUNDATION IS LAID

Eleven years after George Williams and his friends began to meet in his room above the factory, ninety-nine delegates from all over the world traveled to Paris, France, to attend the first world conference of the Young Men's Christian Association. They thought, prayed, debated, and carefully chose each word of a foundation statement which would bear the load of the work to come, anchor the YMCA against unpredictable forces, and prevent the slow creep of decay.

It was at this gathering in 1855 that the original, global purpose statement of the YMCA was agreed upon and adopted. It is known as the Paris Basis.

The Paris Basis boldly states,

The Young Men's Christian Associations seek to unite those young men who, regarding Jesus Christ as their God and Savior, according to the Holy Scriptures, desire to be his disciples in their faith and in their life, and to associate their efforts for the extension of his Kingdom amongst young men.

Any differences of opinion on other subjects, however important in themselves, shall not interfere with the harmonious relations of the constituent members and associates of the World Alliance.[1]

I have traveled to YMCAs on nearly every continent and seen the value this foundation still has today. I have seen grown men in developing countries put their hands over their hearts and with tears recite the words of this mission by memory. I've been to small YMCA huts in the middle of the jungle, conferences of YMCA employees in the villages of India, camps and orphanages, halfway homes and feeding centers, all bearing these four letters, and each pledging to live out the same mission.

In 1973 the Sixth World Council of the YMCA met in Kampala, Uganda, and reaffirmed the Paris Basis as the global mission statement. It was again affirmed in 1998 at Challenge 21, the Fourteenth World Council of YMCAs. You could say that the foundation was evaluated and found solid. Today the Paris Basis is the uncontested current mission of the Young Men's Christian Association. Incredibly, there are more than fourteen thousand global locations which pledge to align themselves with this foundational purpose.

FOUR CORNERS

The Paris Basis very intentionally builds its foundation with four corners: Jesus (God's Son), the Bible (God's Word), disciples (God's followers), and the kingdom (God's mission).

If a foundation is as important to the YMCA as it is to our homes, then we would do well to evaluate and understand its construction a little more deeply.

The Young Men's Christian Associations seek to unite those young men who, regarding Jesus Christ as their God and Savior, according to the Holy Scriptures, desire to be his disciples in their faith and in their life, and to associate their efforts for the extension of his Kingdom amongst young men.

1. JESUS (GOD'S SON)

... regarding Jesus Christ as their God and Savior ...

The Paris Basis says something bold and amazing about the identity of Jesus. It doesn't begin by lifting Jesus up as a model or as the source of the Christian principles that shape many of our associations. (Although He is, and they do.)

Rather than emphasizing any of these profound things, the Paris Basis focuses on Jesus' identity as God and as Savior.

Are these just throwaway words? Religious-speak?

Not if the foundation is carefully crafted. What, then, does it mean to regard Jesus as God?

Because few people think as clearly or say things as well as does C. S. Lewis, why don't we consider his thoughts on the subject? In *Mere Christianity*, Lewis says this:

> *A man who was merely a man and said the sort of things Jesus said would not be a great moral teacher. He would either be a lunatic—on the level with the man who says he is a poached egg—or else he would be the Devil of Hell. You must make your choice. Either this man was, and is, the Son of God, or else a madman or something worse. You can shut him up for a fool, you can spit at him and kill him as a demon or you can fall at his feet and call him Lord and God, but let us not come with any patronizing nonsense about his being a great human teacher.*[2]

Jesus claimed to be the Lord God, the creator and sustainer of our lives. He also claimed to love the whole world, showing the extent of His love by laying down His life for us. The God who is also the Savior, the Creator who entered His creation to rescue us from our mess. If this is true, then it would seem to call for some sort of response from us.

In 1989, Ulrich Parzany represented the YMCA at the Lausanne Conference for World Evangelism. For many years he had served as the general secretary of the German YMCA, and for many more years he had followed Jesus.

Speaking on the topic "The Uniqueness of Christ," he said,

> *The uniqueness of Christ is that in Him the Lord*
> *and Judge of the world has become a human being.*
> *The question, "who is Jesus?" leads to discovering his*
> *uniqueness. The uniqueness of what he said, what he*
> *did, and what happened to him in suffering, crucifixion*
> *and resurrection is to be derived from the uniqueness*
> *of who he is. Why is the death of Jesus the only way to*
> *reconcile men with God? The uniqueness of his death*
> *is not in how he died. Thousands were crucified by*
> *the Romans with the same brutality and cruelty. The*
> *uniqueness of his death is in who he is. The suffering*
> *Lord and Judge of the world takes the place of the lost*
> *sinner. The Judge himself suffers the consequences*
> *of the rebellion and enmity of man against God.*
>
> *It is impossible for us to claim another person's biogra-*
> *phy and history. Guilt is not something which we can*
> *throw away like a dirty shirt. Rebellion against God is*
> *the nature of life. And only the Creator, the Lord and the*
> *Judge of the world, is able to break through the barriers*
> *of space and time in order to take our sinful lives and*
> *crucify them on the Cross, and finish the whole case!*[3]

This kind of love that finishes the case, that rescues, that sees, that offers a future and a hope is very much the same kind of love that so impressed George Williams that he *had* to be part of giving it away to others. This kind of love is a person: Jesus Christ the Lord. He set aside the privilege that would accompany such a station, and out of love came to our level to know us and to save us.

At His birth the angels sang that this was "good news of great joy that will be for all the people. For unto you is born this day in the city of David [not a moral leader, not a great teacher, not a life model but] a Savior, who is Christ the Lord" (Luke 2:10–11 ESV). *Good news for all people.* Do you see how inclusive this is? His arms were stretched out wide. Our doors are open wide.

Years after the Paris Basis was written, at the YMCA World Conference in Mysore, India, leaders from around the world gathered to sharpen, clarify, and summarize the objective of their work. This is how they described it: "The central task of the YMCA is to make Jesus Christ known, believed, trusted, loved, served, and exemplified in every life and in all human relationships."[4]

The name Jesus Christ is certainly well known, but despite that, His person and ministry might be among the most misunderstood in history. Because of that, I'd like to take a moment to push back against two prominent misconceptions about what it means to build a foundation whose cornerstone is Jesus Christ.

Misconception 1: Jesus Is Only for Certain People

As Paul Limbert says in *New Perspectives for the YMCA*, "The blond Jesus with Nordic features who is pictured on the walls of many YMCAs is a pale copy of the young bearded Jewish carpenter who made prophetic announcements in Galilee or the resolute critic who seemed so dangerous to the religious elite of Jerusalem."[5] Jesus of Nazareth was never a white, Western man with a message suited only for some single segment of society.

He was brown. He was poor. He was a refugee. He was homeless. Though innocent, He died as a criminal. He was God come near: Immanuel. He entered into our mess and pain and bondage, offering freedom and generous grace.

Jesus said of himself, "The Spirit of the Lord is on me, because he has anointed me to proclaim good news to the poor. He has sent me to proclaim freedom for the prisoners and recovery of sight for the blind, to set the oppressed free" (Luke 4:18 NIV).

Misconception 2: A Foundation Built on Jesus Is a Foundation Built on Rules

Embedded in the history of Christianity is the idea that Jesus came to establish yet another religious code. This couldn't be further from the truth. Jesus came to invite people into a relationship with their Creator. Only His life, death, and resurrection make this possible.

Because of this, when the Paris Basis builds on the person of Jesus, it is not indicating that a set of Christian regulations be structured into the YMCA. Rather, through relationship, there are expressions of who Jesus is and opportunities to find out more.

Oswald Chambers, Christian leader, author, and WWI YMCA chaplain, understood this. He said, "Christianity is not devotion to work, or to a cause, or a doctrine, but devotion to a Person, the Lord Jesus Christ."[6] Later he cautioned against institutionalizing Jesus or making him into some sort of monument rather than our living salvation. "Today Jesus Christ is being dispatched as the figurehead of a religion, a mere example. He is that, but he is infinitely more; He is salvation itself, He is the Gospel of God."[7]

In summary, there is something incredibly unique about Jesus. He was (and is) more than a teacher, more than a moral leader, and more than a religious figurehead. Any words used to describe Him fall short, as He is infinitely more. But most profoundly, He loves us and offers a type of life in which we can know Him and experience grace, forgiveness, purpose, and an abundance of life through Him. A relationship with Jesus is the foundational corner-stone of the YMCA.

2. THE BIBLE (GOD'S WORD)

... according to the Holy Scriptures ...

The second corner of our foundation is uniting men "according to the Holy Scriptures." Why is this important? Well, if the Paris Basis is the foundation for the YMCA, then the Bible, God's Word, is the foundation for the Paris Basis, and really for all the mission work of the YMCA.

Holy isn't a word you'd hear very often outside of a religious context, but it just means "set apart" or "different." The Bible is a different sort of book. It is special. Comprising sixty-six cohesive books written by forty authors over a span of fifteen hundred years, it is woven together by God. It is His word to us, His enduring love letter. His Word is the signal that yes, the God of the universe has something to say; He wants to communicate. He wants to talk with us.

I've read many good books. The Bible is just different. I read it every day and have for decades. I talk about what I'm reading with friends. On a weekly basis I study it and gather with others to hear from it, to peel back the layers, to drink deeply. This book is the breath of God (2 Tim. 3:16); it is living and active, able to dig down into our souls (Heb. 4:12);

it is profitable for teaching, correction, and training, and it builds up and equips (2 Tim. 3:16–17); it lights my path (Ps. 119:105). No other book has captivated me in this way. No other book is revealed and reveals like God's Word.

Dwight L. Moody, a famous YMCA leader who was once the president of the Chicago association, said this about the Bible: "When I pray, I talk to God, but when I read the Bible, God is talking to me; and it is really more important that God should speak to me than that I should speak to Him. I believe we should know better how to pray if we knew our Bibles better."[8]

With God's Word as a foundation stone, we can bring our questions, longings, sadness, sin, hope, and eagerness to the Lord and hear back consistent, personal, loving truth. I am so glad that those many years ago George Williams and his co-laborers saw fit to build God's Word into the YMCA's foundation.

3. DISCIPLES (GOD'S FOLLOWERS)

... desire to be his disciples in their faith and in their life ...

The third corner of our foundation is discipleship. In ancient times every rabbi had disciples, or students, who were particularly characterized by *being with* the rabbi. This was no Sunday school classroom from 9:00 a.m. to 10:00 a.m. once a week. This was not a packed lecture hall led by an esteemed professor. Ancient discipleship, the kind Jesus offered, was intimate, practical learning that came through living life together. It was a combination of following, learning, and even imitating. You've probably seen this at a micro level at your own YMCA. Every once in a while, there is a favorite soccer coach. (Of course, that's "futbol coach" everywhere in the world except for the United States.) But this well-loved coach is probably someone who is great at the sport, maybe has college or even professional experience, and loves to mix it up with the kids. This coach isn't afraid to get down on the kids' level, and at the same time observe, train, drill, and debrief. When this coach is on a lunch break, the kids want to come too. If the coach wears a certain brand of shoes, the kids want them. There's a confluence of friendship, leadership, love, training, empowering, and mission that invites following.

When Jesus invited people to follow Him as a disciple, it was an invitation to be with Him, to learn from Him, and to become like Him. Discipleship was a day-and-night, year-after-year relationship between Jesus and His followers. They lived their lives together. They were friends.

The Paris Basis indicates that contemporary people are invited to be disciples too, following Jesus in faith and in life. We, like the original disciples, may complicate this a bit, but at root being a disciple of Jesus is simple. (Note: I said simple, not easy.) Following Jesus happens out of faith.

The word faith has been woven into pop culture, redefined a time or two, and substantially diluted, so I'd like to take a moment to describe it. Faith is a deeply biblical concept that marries confidence and dependence with responsive action. When a person believes something to be true and is willing to take a step based on that belief, we'd describe it as faith. Perhaps we might use the word trust to communicate this concept.

Trust is a relational word, and relationship is the context for Jesus' kind of discipleship. He asks his followers to trust Him as they move forward, one step at a time.

Living life by following Jesus has nothing to do with subscribing to a set of rules and regulations, with corresponding consequences and rewards. If it were, we would hardly need to trust and follow *Him*. We could just get really good at following the *rules*. (By the way, this is often called religion.) The kind of faith and following that the Bible speaks of, and that the Paris Basis points to, is rooted in knowing and trusting Jesus.

4. GOD'S KINGDOM (GOD'S MISSION)

... the extension of his Kingdom amongst young men ...

The young men of the YMCA were not observers or mere recipients. They were not people who had been rescued just to sit on the sidelines. Rather they mobilized to share the light they had received. They were participants in "the extension of his Kingdom amongst young men."

What a beautiful thing! Most of the young people of the YMCA will not have books written about them to celebrate their birthdays. Many will not be remembered past their generation. However, each person who has stepped into the mission of the YMCA has stepped into tremendous significance. There is a weightiness and a substance to those who participate in God's kingdom of love.

Think of those people in your life who have loved you well. You were changed, weren't you? Shaped, softened, strengthened. This is what happens, person by person, as the kingdom of love extends among men and women.

The kingdom of God is not like the kingdoms of this world. Those kingdoms operate by an undergirding of rules, brute power, force, and violence. Over the centuries they topple, fall, decay, and are replaced by more rules and more power. In contrast, the kingdom that the Paris Basis references and seeks to expand is a kingdom undergirded by love, sacrifice, and hope. It is stable and growing; it is full of life.

The subject of the kingdom of God is likely too hefty for this little book, but with the help of a few YMCA leaders, I'll try to describe it as the Bible does.

The Reign and Rule of God

Caesar Molebatsi, former president of the Global Alliance of the YMCA, talks about it like this: "The kingdom of God is *His* kingdom, *His* rule, *His* authority. The kingdom deals with the future in that we will only experience the fullness of the kingdom when the King returns. But the kingdom also has a present dimension which we experience and participate in now. The kingdom's values are consistent with the character of the King."[9]

And what is the character of the King? In one word, love. The reign and rule of God is sacrificial and loving. Jesus Christ, who laid down His life for us, leads with justice, mercy, goodness, and grace. When a person or a team or a YMCA seeks to let Jesus lead, the kingdom of God is there.

The Presence of God

Martin Luther King Jr., who was greatly influenced by the YMCA, said, "When we see social relationships controlled everywhere by the principles which Jesus illustrated in life—trust, love, mercy, and altruism—then we shall know that the kingdom of God is here."[10]

The kingdom is anywhere that Jesus is. A class, a team, a hunger initiative, a YMCA board meeting are so much more than human efforts when we invite God into the mix. When He is there, we are part of His kingdom work.

The Transforming Power of God in Action

Andrew Murray, the beloved author, was the first president of the YMCA of South Africa. He has this to say about God's transforming power:

> *Come, and however feeble you feel, just wait in His presence ... come with all that is dark and cold in you into the sunshine of God's holy, omnipotent love, and sit and wait there, with the one thought: Here I am, in the sunshine of His love. As the sun does its work in the weak one who seeks its rays, God will do His work in you.*[11]

God's kingdom brings transformation to this broken world. God's power, poured out in love, changes everything. Relationships are reconciled, hearts are healed, crooked things are made straight, hope grows out of despair, anxiety gives way to peace. Jesus' love wins.

I'm sure you've stood on a beach, lakeside, or even at a pond and tossed a rock into the water. If the water is still, you can see the power of one well-aimed rock. Concentric circles ripple out, on and on. The energy from the impact continues even well past the time that we can see it on the surface.

Jesus entered this world and announced, "The kingdom of God is here." The impact is still rippling out today. When we mentor a kid, when we clean up a road, when we sit with a lonely person, we are part of the rippling kingdom of God, which will ripple on until it is fulfilled in the new heavens and the new earth.

In the past two hundred years, countless unnamed and seemingly unnoticed men and women have sought to expand God's kingdom of love through their service at the YMCA. Even small efforts matter greatly in this kingdom because God's love never fails.

I hope that this is much more than an exploration of the foundation laid by the Paris Basis; may it also be an encouragement that the kingdom work many of you are doing is incredibly significant.

UNITY AMID DIVERSITY

The second paragraph of the Paris Basis says,

Any differences of opinion on other subjects, however important in themselves, shall not interfere with the harmonious relations of the constituent members and associates of the World Alliance.

Over the years, I've noticed that YMCA teaching and training on the Paris Basis tends to give lots of attention to getting the first paragraph right, but then ignores the second paragraph. If the first paragraph focuses on foundational corners that are forever and unwavering, the second paragraph is meant to give freedom inside that framework.

The CEO of my YMCA, Chris Johnson, finds a lot of freedom in that second paragraph. He loves to point out that the global mission statement (the Paris Basis) gives him four corners to build on boldly and gives him the opportunity to say, "There are a whole lot of secondary issues which we just refuse to fight about."

Almost everyone likes the idea of unity. A lot. But in every circle of life, and throughout history, people have found unity hard to build and preserve. Perhaps the greatest path to unity can be discovered within the YMCA's foundational Bible verse. It is carved in stone logos, printed on camp T-shirts, and painted on YMCA banners all over the world.

The theme verse of our movement is a prayer for unity. That's significant. In a tender, tearful moment, Jesus prayed for all the people who would ever follow Him, asking "that they may all be one ..." (John 17:21 ESV).

Jesus prayed for unity.

So how do we shape a culture in which a diverse group of people can experience the type of unity that He was praying for? Jesus reveals part of the answer as he continues: "... just as you, Father, are in me, and I in you, that they also may be in us, so that the world may believe that you have sent me" (John 17:21 ESV). Jesus points to a deep connection with Him as the source of this unity.

A. W. Tozer talks about unity in this way: "Has it ever occurred to you that one hundred pianos all tuned to the same fork are automatically tuned to each other? They are of one accord by being tuned, not to each other, but to another standard to which each one must individually bow."[12]

A personal connection with Jesus is the source of our unity. If we learn to love, serve, and care like Jesus did, tuning our hearts to His, we can experience the kind of unity that brings great peace and power to our purpose.

———————

A few years ago, YMCA leaders gathered together in the garden of Gethsemane. In a quiet, holy moment we prayed in the very place that Jesus prayed over two thousand years ago. We prayed that the YMCA would fulfill the heart cry of its original founder, Jesus. We prayed for Unity. We prayed that "we would all be one".

CHAPTER 7
BUILDING WELL

The foundation is solid. The four corners are strong, and because of its strength, the YMCA can support flexibility. Over the years, YMCAs around the world have worked through how the Paris Basis can be contextualized to address contemporary needs. We want to discover how this foundational statement can be translated into accurate, accessible language that readily says, "This is what we do."

And what is it that we do? Are we primarily a health club? Are we an aging institution with nothing unique to offer?

Paul Limbert, the general secretary of the World Alliance for a decade, once told the story of a YMCA in New England whose building was distinguished by large electric letters spelling out Y-M-C-A along the rooftop. Far and wide, across the city, the YMCA was illuminated, easy to locate, and a welcoming beacon.

At some point, however, the lights powering the C went out, and the sign remained that way for several weeks.

For many, this is a parable of the situation of YMCAs in the United States. People are asking, What has happened to the "C" in YMCA? Have the lights that once seemed to make the Christian character of this movement clear and visible gone out in this technological age ...? There is no simple answer to this question. It is reassuring to know that a number of thoughtful leaders of the YMCA movement are raising even more searching questions, such as, What does it mean to be a significant Christian Association on the American scene?[1]

This question is no less significant today than it was when Limbert first posed it.

If we don't consider what it means to build on our foundation, and don't press into how that foundation supports today's work, the YMCA will default to being merely a family friendly gym.

Why settle for such a limited and lackluster identity, when in truth we were built to be a movement radiating Christ's love out into darkness?

Let's look at some of the ways the YMCA has built well on its foundation.

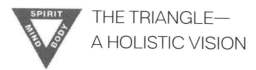

THE TRIANGLE—
A HOLISTIC VISION

Over the years, there have been no less than eight YMCA logos. (And I must say, as the husband of a graphic designer, I am in awe of the simple power of a good logo!) Except for the first one, each YMCA logo has incorporated a triangle. This streamlined symbol speaks to layers of missional meaning at the YMCA.

Most simply, the equilateral sides of the triangle each represent a distinct element of what the early founders believed it meant to be human. They are body, mind, and spirit. Today we would describe this as a holistic view of a person.

Despite the common perception that the YMCA is just a gym and swim, the YMCA has always been interested in the whole person. We are focused not exclusively on the body but on the mind and spirit as well. Now, the truth is that many YMCAs emphasize the physical. As a result, we are one of the most successful, extensive physical fitness platforms in the world. But a triangle with only one side is not a triangle. It's just a line.

What if we made the other two sides of our triangle equally strong, so the three sides together formed a truly robust, holistic mission? What if along with physical fitness, we offered support for mental health and mental health awareness? What if we could supplement education where it is needed? What if we provided chaplains, resources, and classes to nurture spiritual growth? Many more YMCAs than you might imagine are already strengthening their holistic mission and are making real, significant impact on their communities as a result.

THE KAMPALA PRINCIPLES AND CHALLENGE 21

As the YMCA has stretched from the nineteenth century into the twenty-first, there have been several significant assessments and affirmations of its foundation. They are the Kampala Principles and Challenge 21.

These documents are attached, in their entirety, at the end of this book. Men and women from YMCAs around the world prayerfully crafted each word. These statements are built to offer freedom within a framework.

The framework is the Paris Basis and its expression is essentially that Christ is the center of the movement.

Within this framework, each YMCA around the world has the freedom to assess its own community's needs and to express its purpose in a manner that most clearly serves those needs.

CHANGE AGENTS: INDIVIDUALS WHO MADE A DIFFERENCE

I'd rather see a sermon than hear one any day. As a pastor, I invest a lot of time in preparing and sharing sermons. Over the years, I've come to realize that my life speaks louder than any message I deliver with words. Likewise, mission statements are often easier to read in people's lives than when they're printed on documents and banners. Let's look at the lives of those early change agents who shaped the YMCA.

DWIGHT L. MOODY

Much like George Williams, D. L. Moody left his family farm and ventured to the city to find his way. He became a Christian in 1855 at the age of eighteen. Two years later, instead of working at a Chicago shoe store as he had intended, he was sleeping under a staircase, working as a janitor so he could volunteer at the YMCA.

The people around him were poor. Moody saw their needs and made it his mission—and the mission of the YMCA—to meet them. He delivered necessities: coal, food, and clothing. As he went from house to house with these bundles, he prayed for people and offered, if they were interested, to read the Bible with them.[2]

If Moody lived among the poor, nearby were people living in even more excruciating poverty and need. Chicago's "Little Hell" neighborhood was dangerous and depraved. Churches and social services would not step foot inside its boundaries. Police stayed out. But the children broke Moody's heart, and he was determined to bring the YMCA into Little Hell.

He earned the nickname "Crazy Moody,"[3] because he would load up a horse with baskets stuffed full of bread, coal, and blankets and ride into Little Hell, meeting and serving anyone he could find. His acquaintances couldn't understand it. Soon he began raising money to rent out a saloon on Sundays. With pockets full of candy and pennies, he invited kids into a safe, fun, loving space for two hours each week. He must have been young enough to remember what it was like to be a kid: he taught them from the Bible in five-minute increments, each followed by a few minutes of rowdiness and wrestling and then singing.[4] Over and over, truth and love, candy and wrestling, sugar and singing. You may not have wanted D. L. Moody to volunteer in your church's nursery. But if you would have entered that saloon in Little Hell, you would've had to say, "The kingdom of God is here!"

God used this "Sunday school" in amazing ways. By the end of 1860, fifteen hundred kids were coming each week. News about this YMCA mission school spread so widely that even Abraham Lincoln came to visit.[5] Moody took the bright light of the YMCA into the darkness of Little Hell.

ANTHONY BOWEN

When Anthony Bowen passed away, he didn't want his death to be marked by a formal ceremony. Nevertheless, more than two hundred carriages followed along to the cemetery.[6]

Born into slavery in 1809, he purchased his own freedom twenty-one years later for $425. Shortly afterward he and his wife moved to Washington, D.C., and in 1853, only two years after the first YMCA opened its doors in the United States, Bowen founded the first YMCA open to black men. His passion was to see black men advance spiritually, socially, and educationally.[7]

His home was part of the Underground Railroad, as well as the first location of the "Sunday Evening School"—an organization in which he taught young black men to read, to write, and to study the Bible.[8]

Bowen founded St. Paul's A.M.E. Church, a community that not only worshiped together on Sundays but used their building as a school for escaped slaves and as a stop on the Underground Railroad. When he died, his only request was that his friends work to make the mission of St. Paul's succeed.[9]

In 1908 the YMCA chapter Bowen founded constructed its first building. It is still an active YMCA in Washington, D.C., today.

Anthony Bowen made his mark as a member of the Redeemer's kingdom—the realm of the One who sets the captive free. Bowen believed men were created for freedom and dignity in body, and in mind and soul as well. His life's work was freeing, strengthening, and empowering his fellow men to go out and do the same.

OSWALD CHAMBERS

When Oswald Chambers arrived in Cairo to serve the British Commonwealth troops, he immediately set up a YMCA hut: a spiritual gathering place for battle-weary soldiers. They had been out to war for a little more than a year. Those who lived would fight for three more years, until the World War ended in 1918. "Hut" is a bit of a misnomer, because not long after Chambers and his wife, Biddie, began hosting teas and Bible studies there, it was packed out with hundreds and hundreds of soldiers.

Perhaps it was the combination of the this couple's passion for Jesus and love for people that drew those young men. Night after night Chambers taught the Bible. And when men turned up to eat home-cooked meals, they were always welcomed regardless of their spiritual interest. "They came to eat, not to hear a sermon," Chambers said. "There's a meeting later tonight if they want to stay and hear someone preach."[10] It turns out, they did want to stay.

"Reports began filtering into Y.M.C.A. headquarters that soldiers whom no one could accuse of being religious turned out night after night to study the Bible."[11]

Whether in the hut or on the field, tending to the wounded, Chambers, on behalf of the Young Men's Christian Association, loved these men well. He built on a firm foundation and created a strong platform for all of us who would come after.

JOHN R. MOTT

In 1946 John R. Mott was awarded the Nobel Peace Prize "for his contribution to the creation of a peace-promoting religious brotherhood across national boundaries."[12] What was this international peace-promoting brotherhood? The YMCA, of course! Mott served the YMCA for forty-three years, including many years as the general secretary and president of the World Council.

When he accepted the Nobel Peace Prize, Mott said that the "outstanding, unfailing, and abiding secret of all great and truly enduring leadership" was summed up when Jesus said, "He who would be greatest among you shall be the servant of all."[13] Mott contributed a great many things to the

YMCA, particularly his leadership in promoting Christian unity. But his understanding of the deep value of loving others through service shines most brightly in a world where many leaders seek the spotlight.

While Mott may best be remembered as a Nobel laureate, one of my favorite stories comes from long before that time. When he was a rising sophomore at Cornell, Mott, charismatic and driven, propelled the university chapter of the YMCA to become the largest on any campus in the United States.[14] In that same year, 1886, his chapter nominated him to attend a month-long summer conference for students, hosted by D. L. Moody.

After the nomination, he wrote this to his parents: "Dear Parents, I have made the first decision of any importance which I have ever made without your advice; but it was no matter of self; it was of God from beginning to end—and I do not think you will object to my decision. Mark me when I say that it was not the solicitation of the Association, nor the prompting of my pastor which led me to this decision, but conscience alone. Your affectionate son, John R. Mott."[15]

That summer, Mott was one of 250 young people from eighty-nine colleges and universities who gathered to study the Bible, learn about missions, and plan how to impact their schools when they returned in the fall.[16]

It became clear that a passion was building among the students for people across the world to know Christ. Mott and many others prayed day and night that the Lord would raise up people to love and serve every tribe and nation.

Kids who grow up in church today likely have many opportunities to go on service trips, or short-term mission trips. Just this week, my oldest son left for a country in Africa with YWAM—Youth with a Mission. When John Mott and his friends gathered that summer to pray, there was no such model. There were no organizations encouraging, training, and mobilizing students to do the kind of service and mission work that make such an impact in our world today.

At the closing prayer, ninety-nine students gathered one last time and asked the Lord to use them, to send them. As they prayed, one last man entered the room and knelt. This moment, which came to be known as the "Mt. Hermon Hundred," was a galvanizing point in the organization of the Student Volunteer Movement.[17] In 1898 Mott, with several other students, launched the SVM as an arm of the YMCA.[18] The student mission movement that we know today grew out of this movement.

K.T. PAUL

In 1912 K. T. Paul was tapped by John Mott to become the national secretary of the YMCA of India. India's was one of the earliest global YMCAs, and Paul was the earliest indigenous leader. While his legacy is large, two pieces made a particular impact. One was an eager desire to see a truly Indian Christian movement develop in his country, and specifically in the YMCA. He wanted a truly Christian foundation, built upon with flexible forms that reflected the realities and cultures of the communities he served.[19]

The other piece of Paul's unique legacy was the Rural Reconstruction movement. Burdened for the poorest of the poor in rural India, Paul leveraged his position at the YMCA to train people in agricultural practices, to found a cooperative bank, and to implement a wide-reaching literacy program.

Some of the specific plans implemented by the Rural Reconstruction movement were to:

- foster habits of good stewardship

- increase the earning power of the villager by making agricultural opportunities available and financing affordable

- enrich the social side of life by means of excursions and festivals for villagers

- attend to their physical culture by providing facilities for sports and gymnastics[20]

K.T. Paul was truly concerned about the spirit, mind and body of the people that he served.

I have personally had the privilege of dedicating many YMCAs in rural villages throughout India. As I have seen community after community transformed by the love of God and the work of the YMCA, I am thankful for this man who lived on mission and served holistically.

HENRY DUNANT

Henry Dunant was raised to care for "the least of these" (Matt. 25:40 NIV). As a child, he went with his mother to tend to poor and sick people who lived in his hometown of Geneva, Switzerland. He followed that tender passion into adulthood, continuing to visit the poor and the sick regularly. Dunant went on to start the Red Cross, win a Nobel Peace Prize, and—not insignificantly—spend twenty years serving the YMCA. In 1852 Dunant rallied a group of friends and co-laborers to establish the YMCA in Geneva.

Dunant cared for the hurting and the overlooked, but he was also passionate about the organization he had helped to establish. His lasting imprint on the YMCA was two-fold: that its meetings would retain intimate, spiritual excitement, and that it would be welcoming and inclusive rather than nationalistic. To that end, he was instrumental in launching the World Alliance of YMCAs.[21]

JAMES NAISMITH

In 1891 James Naismith was given an interesting assignment by his professor at the YMCA International Training School in Massachusetts. His professor asked the class to work on creating some new games, particularly those which could be played indoors in the winter. Naismith went to work, with an idea of combining elements of familiar games into something completely new. After serious consideration, Naismith drafted a list of rules, nailed two peach baskets to either side of the gymnasium, and divided his class of eighteen men into two teams to try out the new game: basketball.[22]

When Naismith applied to the YMCA training school, he was asked a question: "What is the work of a YMCA Physical Director?" His answer expressed his commitment to Jesus and his passion for sports: "To win men to the Master through the gym."[23] To this day, the YMCA is one of the best places in the world to encounter men and women who love basketball and love Jesus. What a privilege to continue in the legacy of winning people to the Master through the gym.

CHANGE AGENTS: ASSOCIATIONS THAT MADE A DIFFERENCE

Not only were individual men and women stirred with the calling of ministry through the YMCA, but associations were driven by a vision of ministry. Countless unnamed men and women loved God, loved their fellow human beings, and out of that love sought to work through the YMCA to meet pressing needs.

In 1867 a major cholera epidemic broke out in Chicago and it was the YMCA who stepped in to aid the city's "untouchables," as volunteers nursed more than sixty families and performed last rites for the dead.[24] The same Chicago association realized that the needs of the city were great and that many men were homeless. Therefore in 1916 the YMCA built a hotel that had 1,821 bedrooms and was nineteen stories high. The purpose of the hotel was to provide a place for men to stay as they transitioned from unemployment to employment. The president of the association at the time, Loring Wilbur Messer, reflected, "The greatest sight in the world is a man. The saddest sight in the world is a wreck of a man. The noblest work in the world is the building of a man."[25]

During the American Civil War, the YMCA determined to find ways to meet the spiritual and physical needs of soldiers. Fifteen YMCAs banded together. They organized five thousand volunteers to distribute 1,446,748 Bibles and 1,370,953 hymnbooks. They preached 58,308 sermons and conducted 77,744 prayer meetings. They delivered hot bread and coffee to the soldiers on the battlefield and wrote letters for the wounded soldiers. Over and over they asked, "How can I serve you?" It was often a YMCA volunteer who would pen the final words to a loved one from the lips of a dying soldier. In addition to this, the YMCA opened schools for uneducated soldiers and performed many other acts of compassion.[26]

A woman whose name you've probably never heard—Annie Witenmeyer—was burdened to serve men on the battlefield. She gathered 110 women and went onto the field, setting up kitchens to serve healthy meals to soldiers. In a tough battle moment, the YMCA said, "We're not staying away. We are entering this dangerous situation. We will serve."

In 1869 the railroad that connected the eastern United States to the West was finally completed. Many pioneering young men traveled the country in search of adventure. The YMCA saw need in the lives of these young men and set up many railroad associations. Bible classes, clean beds, and hot baths were offered at any time of the day for these railroad pioneers.[27]

While the roots of the YMCA are in England, it quickly grew into a global movement based on sharing the hope and love of Jesus Christ. Today there are YMCAs in 120 countries.

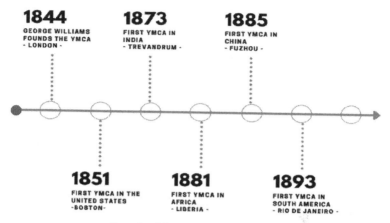

1844
GEORGE WILLIAMS
FOUNDS THE YMCA
- LONDON -

1873
FIRST YMCA IN
INDIA
- TREVANDRUM -

1885
FIRST YMCA IN
CHINA
- FUZHOU -

1851
FIRST YMCA IN THE
UNITED STATES
-BOSTON-

1881
FIRST YMCA IN
AFRICA
- LIBERIA -

1893
FIRST YMCA IN
SOUTH AMERICA
- RIO DE JANEIRO -

Growth of the YMCA movement[28]

From passionate evangelists riding horseback into cities, to wartime huts, to homeless shelters, to basketball leagues, to lunch hour prayer meetings, God has undeniably used this movement to shine the light of Jesus Christ around the world.

The YMCA is still asking how we can serve our communities. Are there kids who are vulnerable? Are there people who are hungry? Do people need childcare, financial literacy, or career coaching? Could we help with a community garden or a neighborhood cleanup effort? I have a challenge for you. Just like those who came before us, those who built on a strong foundation, will you ask yourself the question, every day, "How can I serve?"

CHAPTER 8

CHRISTIAN PRINCIPLES

As powerful as these stories are, some of you may still wonder about the C in the YMCA. You may have thought, "Hey, wait a minute. YMCA stands for the Young Men's Christian Association. But we're not just for the young anymore. We're not just for men anymore. Why not say, 'And we're not Christian anymore?'"

THE YMCA/JCC OF GREATER TOLEDO

My good friend Josh Heaston used to work in a YMCA that operated in conjunction with a JCC (Jewish Community Center). It was a great collaboration in many ways, and Josh's time there offered some interesting observations about what it means to operate on a foundation, out of mission, and out of identity. It impacted him so much that to this day he carries a YMCA/JCC key chain around with him.

Josh has spent his entire adult life serving and working in YMCAs. His passion for loving and caring for people runs deep and is anchored into his heart for the Y.

Josh's own work of thinking through mission—what it means and how to apply it—began the first day he stepped foot in a YMCA as an after-school program employee. Here's how he tells the story.

I started my career with YMCA/JCC of Greater Toledo in 2000. I was doing before-and-after-school care. It was kind of like a youth counselor position. We played Connect Four, helped with homework, and threw a football around. Now, when you get hired into a Y, they send you to a new staff orientation. That's where I learned the seventeen words "to put Christian principles into practice through programs that build healthy spirit, mind, and body for all." And I thought, "Well, I'm not a genius, but this sounds like a Christian mission statement." You know, it's got the word Christian in there, it talks about principles, and it mentions our spirits. So I stopped by my boss's office afterward and asked, "How are we putting Christian principles into practice and building healthy spirits in these kids?"

She looked at me and said, "We're not doing that."

In my mind, I was thinking, "What kind of organization did I just sign up for? You sent me to a new staff training, you told me the mission statement, and then when I asked about it, you told me that you're not doing it."

So I asked, "What would you think if I tried?" I thought
maybe we could just read a Bible story to the kids or
do a skit or sing a song or teach them the meaning of
a Christian principle. We could just do something.
It wouldn't be one hundred percent of the program.
We'd still play Connect Four and help with homework
and throw the football. But what if I just slid five
minutes of something Christian in there? She agreed
to let me give it a try.

When Josh began to move his YMCA into alignment with the mission statement, people loved it. Parents sought him out to thank him for introducing a "healthy spirit" focus to their kids. Over the past two decades, his vision and passion have developed into a concrete, reproducible platform for loving, caring for, and serving the spiritual needs of staff and members of many YMCAs across the United States.

AUDIENCE AND IDENTITY

Josh's formative YMCA experience was intertwined with the JCC. This is significant for several reasons, but perhaps most clearly because it taught Josh the distinction between audience and identity. He says this:

The JCC is not ashamed or afraid to be Jewish. They
post their dietary laws, they keep a kosher environment,

they close on Jewish holidays, they say "shalom" when they answer the phone. They are proud of their Jewish heritage. It makes the JCC special and unique. If the JCC is not afraid or ashamed to be Jewish, why should we be ashamed or afraid to be Christian? But you just have to figure out how to do that. You don't beat people over the head with a Bible, you don't make them feel bad, you don't preach at them.

Reflecting on this, Josh asked,

Can we be intentional about our Christian mission? We wrestled with that for awhile and concluded, it's okay to be who you are. Let's just make sure we have a genuine respect for those who are different.

Here's the thing, our mission statement says, "to put Christian principles into practice through programs that build healthy spirit, mind, and body for all." Is "for all" referring to our audience or to our identity? Sit with that question for a minute. Is "for all" referring to our audience or to our identity?

*When I answer that question, "for all" means our audience. We want to impact everybody. That doesn't mean we believe just anything or do just anything or say just anything. Our identity is rooted in that word **Christian**.*

Christian is still in our name for a reason. We believe that Christian principles can have an amazing, encouraging, uplifting effect on all people. So our identity is Christian, and we aren't ashamed of that or afraid of that, but our audience is absolutely anyone who wants to walk through our doors.

CHRISTIAN PRINCIPLES IN PRACTICE

So how are Christian principles put into practice at local YMCAs? What does it look like?

My YMCA—the Countryside YMCA—builds twelve Christian principles into our everyday work and relationships: respect, caring, responsibility, honesty, faith, empowerment, servanthood, forgiveness, hope, grace, peace, and love. We look for ways to live them out, to weave them throughout our communities.

We offer more than four hundred classes, clubs, leagues, and lessons and see these as four hundred unique opportunities to put Christian principles into practice. The goals of our basketball and flag football leagues are less about Olympic dreams and more about teaching our kids to treat a referee with respect or to care for teammates. Often we begin our exercise classes with an optional prayer. Our coaches are trained to incorporate a Christian principle into a huddle time during each practice.

In addition to our programs, we shape our environment so that it communicates our values. Quotes about the principles decorate our walls. We offer a chapel stocked with hundreds of resources on how to put Christian principles into practice in marriage, parenting, and work. Outside on the grounds, we are building a nature trail with twelve stopping points, each dedicated to one of our Christian principles. Members can walk along, stopping at each station to creatively put the principle into practice through a thought, exercise or an activity.

At Countryside we have a really great childcare program. We serve kids from six months through sixth grade, with a creative curriculum that incorporates our principles. Each month, the teachers incorporate a Christian principle into the curriculum. February is "love" month, and that's not only because of Valentine's Day. We want our kids to learn how to count and say the alphabet. But even more than that, we want our kids to learn that they are loved by God and loved by their YMCA teachers. We want them to learn how to show love to the people in their lives.

Christian principles are incorporated into our programs, environment, and classrooms, but in essence they are the heartbeat of the people who serve Countryside YMCA. Some of the most impactful ways Christian principles play out are unplanned and behind the scenes.

A few weeks ago a new guy stopped by the gym at the Countryside YMCA for some pickup basketball. Halfway into the game he collided with another player and had to retreat to the stands as his ribs were injured. One of our volunteers, a man who is at the YMCA to live on mission, saw this happen. He walked over, sat down, and introduced himself. They talked about basketball, he asked if his ribs were ok, and they watched the rest of the game together. As they were getting to know each other, the volunteer showed a great interest in this young man. "Tell me your story. I want to hear it," he said.

It turns out this guy had stopped by the YMCA that day not just to play basketball but with some hopes of making a new start in his life. Having been shown the smallest amount of regard and care, he opened up and shared his need. Our volunteer was empathetic. "If it's all right with you, I'd love to pray for you," he said. The man was grateful for the prayers, and they bowed their heads together courtside. The two stayed in touch, and a few weeks later our YMCA was able to be part of that man's new start by providing some needed furniture for his apartment.

Year round, people of all ages, races, and creeds can walk into a YMCA built on Christian principles and expect to experience kindness, respect, and an overflow of the person of Jesus. We are trying to aim well at the right target.

THE ANNUAL PLEDGE

Twelve Christian principles. A faith-based identity. A Christ-centered mission statement. The unobscured truth is that the YMCA is indeed an organization founded on the hope that young men and women of all ages and races would be introduced to the transforming love of Jesus Christ.

The good work that so many dedicated staff and volunteers give themselves to every day has been shaped and informed by this mission for nearly two centuries.

Over and over this foundation has been evaluated and affirmed: the triangle, the Paris Basis, Challenge 21, the Kampala Principles, the lives of so many men and women who built upon the foundation. This reevaluation and reaffirmation is not ancient history either. Every single year—this year—the CEOs of every YMCA in the United States sign a pledge which in part reads,

> *We, the undersigned, in applying for a listing in the official roster of duly organized Young Men's Christian Associations, certify the following:*
>
> *That our association accepts and supports the statement of purpose of the Young Men's Christian Associations of the United States of America, which is:* **The Young Men's Christian Association we regard as being in its essential genius a worldwide fellowship united by**

a common loyalty to Jesus Christ for the purpose of developing Christian personality and building a Christian society.[1]

This document, the Annual Pledge, is on my desk as I write. It must be signed and returned to the Certification and Membership Standards office at the National YMCA of the USA. I am inspired by its words and challenged by its boldness. Though the application of this statement will certainly look different in various contexts, my passionate plea is that YMCAs would remain true and authentic to the pledge we all sign.

Relatively few organizations succeed, standing the test of time, remaining effective in terms of their goals. Yet the YMCA has existed, expanded, and effected change for close to two centuries. I believe with all my heart that this is because of the strength, truth, and consistency of its mission and aim. Let us not strip the strength of the YMCA. Let us not allow our aim to drift.

The YMCA has the potential to be fourteen thousand lighthouses strong. Oh, the impact we might have on the world. But our aim must be true!

More than one hundred years ago, the president and the general secretary of the International YMCA looked to the future and prayed that the generations of YMCA leaders yet to come would be true to their aim and unwavering in their mission.

They spoke to us.

They wrote to us and challenged us not only to be true to our mission but to so tether that mission to ourselves that we would be missionaries: change agents living on mission in this world.

Written to future leaders of the YMCA, June 1894

Our fellow workers of the ages to come, whom, though yet unborn, we greet today, may have yet to record yet nobler achievements, if only they never forget that the one secret of success is the life of the Spirit of God in the heart, and that love of souls which makes every Christian a missionary. Without any outward aids our forefathers succeeded, because they had in their hearts this fire of first love, and without this, no commodious buildings, no wise organizations, no staff of able secretaries can keep our Association from going to decay. Nothing can take the place of spiritual life, and spiritual life is one long victory. Courage then, brothers of today and tomorrow! On our knees at the foot of the Cross, where we swear allegiance to our Divine Master, let us ask without ceasing for a renewal of that baptism of life out of which has arisen, among countless other blessed institutions, our Young Men's Christian Association.

—President G. Tophel
—General Secretary C. H. Fermaud[2]

PART THREE
THE MOVEMENT

CHAPTER 9
SPREADING LIGHT

There is a scene in *The Lord of the Rings: The Return of the King* when Gandalf the Wizard assigns Pippin the Hobbit to do a critical task. He sends him off to light the beacon. The beacon is an immense stone tower set atop a cliff. At the very top is a wide, round, stone floor piled high with cut wood. In essence it is a massive torch with a mighty purpose. When the wood catches fire and blazes from the mountaintop, men across Middle Earth will see it and in turn light their beacons. Lights will flicker for miles and miles along the horizon, illuminating the darkness and calling men to fight for good.[1]

One beacon, blazing, creates a movement of light.

The YMCA is a story of such a movement. Let's go back again and take a look at that stone pillar at 72 St. Paul's Churchyard.

FROM ITS BEGINNING

IN THIS PLACE

INSPIRED OF GOD

THE ASSOCIATION GREW

TO ENCOMPASS THE WORLD[2]

Inspired by God, a beacon was lit. Its light shone out to many, who in turn were moved to light their own beacons. This light has grown to encompass the world.

In this chapter, I would love to introduce you to some of the beautiful, bright lights shining today in the YMCA. These are men and women from all over the world who are living the mission and inspiring others to do the same.

John, a close friend and follower of Jesus, closed his book on the story of Jesus by saying, "Now there are also many other things that Jesus did. Were every one of them to be written, I suppose that the world itself could not contain the books that would be written" (John 21:25 ESV).

I feel that way about the YMCA's stories. How many pages would it take to capture the moments, big and small, that have built the story of the past two hundred years? Allow me to share just a few of these moments, these stories, these beacons of light.

CAESAR MOLEBATSI

In 1998 a man named Caesar Molebatsi was the president of the World Council of the YMCA. He developed the direction and language of Challenge 21, one of the anchors of our modern mission. It is rather remarkable that he was involved in such a thing, because at the time that Caesar was invited into YMCA leadership, he was still barred from entering most of the YMCA facilities in his home country. He wasn't welcome because he was black in South Africa.

Recently, he told me a bit of his story, and I'd like to share it here.

After I became president of the YMCA, I had a strong desire to reach out to the white leaders of apartheid YMCAs. I wanted to spend time with them as people. We couldn't meet in their YMCAs, so we met in all kinds of crazy places: train stations, fields, you name it. During this outreach and reconciliation effort, I encountered a man who ran one of the most segregated and racist branches of the YMCA.

Funny enough, this man was in the habit of memorizing Scripture. He would always talk about Scripture and talk about his practice of memorizing Scripture, so after we met, I challenged him. "Let's memorize Scripture together!" In addition, I learned that he loved to fish. I asked him to teach me to fish. "Okay, fine," he said. We started to build a bit of a relationship around the Word of God and fishing.

One Christmas, I was taking a busload of kids from a black YMCA to go camping at the oceanfront. It was late, and after much driving around, we could not find a place to stay. As a last-ditch effort, I drove to the YMCA compound at Richards Bay. This YMCA was led by the YMCA general secretary: my fishing and Scripture "friend."

The kids and I were met by security at the gate. There was no way that they were going to let us in there. I spoke with a guard. "It's fine that we can't come in," I said. "But would you please call the YMCA general secretary and tell him that I'm here?"

While the guards quibbled with me, one of the young people on the bus called a friend who was working for the national newspaper. "Our friend Caesar is here, now, at the gate of this Y, and they won't let him in. This will be a good story for you to publish. Come on out—do this story!"

The newspaper arrived just as the general secretary came out to speak with me. "Look," I said, "I know I can't come in. But you're going to go national now. You and your YMCA are going to be in the news." He just looked at me. I continued. "I'm prepared to ask my friends not to avoid writing the story but to write it with a different ending. Yes, it's an ugly story, but we can create a different ending. I *want* it to have a different ending."

"What do you mean?" he asked.

"Let's go fishing," I answered.

He came out and we went fishing. Along the shore that night, as we fished side by side and looked out over the ocean, I told him my story.

I told him that when I was a young teen, an Afrikaans man purposely ran me down in his car as I walked along the road. That I had spent months in the hospital as a result. That I had lost my leg. That I had burned with hatred against white men, and that my heart had hardened with bitterness.

I also told him that God met me in that place of hatred and bitterness and despair. Yes, a white man ran me down and left me for dead. But my surgeon, a kind, skilled, and faithful man—also Afrikaans—looked after me as if I were his own child. Although I never knew his name, he gave me a Bible. After five months I left the hospital to rehabilitate at my uncle's farm, and I read that Bible cover to cover under the orange trees. I came to know some of who this God is— this God who created us all. But I still needed to be challenged to lay down my anger and bitterness. That same year

I made a new friend: a young man who had suffered in many ways, just as much as I had. He was different than I was, though. He had peace and purpose. He knew Jesus.

It was at that point, after the accident, after months in the hospital, and after a year on the farm, that I trusted Jesus with my life and gave myself to Him. God reached down and truly saved me.

The moon was high over the horizon by the time we were finished fishing, and by the time I had told the whole story to my "friend."

"God freed me from my bitterness and anger and hatred, and here I am now," I said. He broke down and cried.

Walking back through the brush, I said, "I know I can't come to your YMCA ..."

"No. You come. You and the kids come to my YMCA."

So we went back to his YMCA. As we approached the guard house and the vanload of sleeping kids, I said, "If the police come and arrest us, that's fine."

He looked at me decisively and said, "I will go to jail with you."

This story, which started out so ugly, this story about

"exposing the racism of this man and his segregated YMCA" ended with the same man inviting me to come to his YMCA and pledging that if needed, he would go to prison with me.

So it was that in many ways, God worked through the YMCA in South Africa to bring about reconciliation and hope, to build love and trust and to repair many broken things.

As much as we are having discussions and even arguments about faith today, I'm telling you now that if we were not being driven by our faith in Christ and our understanding of God's standards of righteousness and mercy and justice, if we were not driven by the love of Christ, we would not have gone on like that. The YMCA wouldn't have been a vehicle for real change. Definitely not. But because we are passionate about these things, we were prepared.

The YMCA once again became the standard bearer, if you will. It became a signpost to the kingdom of God in terms of justice and righteousness, and therefore everything we did was embedded in our understanding of what was demanded of us in terms of God's will.

Powerful. Beautiful. Significant.

The YMCA has been a beacon and vehicle for real change so many times in her history. May it be so again.

ERIC ELLSWORTH

Eric Ellsworth is the CEO of the YMCA of the Cayman Islands. He is known for his kindness and his contagious joy. Before this position, his visionary leadership energized the establishment of multiple YMCAs in the Indianapolis area.

To one kid, though, Eric is known as the man who rescued him.

It had been a long week, and Eric was home, grateful to rest and relax. He had changed into sweats, eaten dinner, and was settling in for the evening. He wasn't quite able to settle, though. He sat on the couch, restless. Something was stirring in his heart. Eric had the strong sense that he should get up, get back in the car, and drive downtown to check on one of the YMCAs. It seemed so random. The YMCA was one he rarely visited on the weekend, especially after 10:00 p.m. It hardly made sense to get up and go there *immediately*. The part of him that was enjoying the couch reasoned, "This is inconvenient," and "I'm already exhausted!" and "A drive will only make me more tired." Yet deep in his heart Eric felt God was trying to get his attention. He had learned over a lifetime to listen to the voice of the Lord.

Eric jumped in his car and drove out from the suburbs toward the city.

Light was pouring out of every window, and groups of laughing kids were bursting in and out of the doors. Eric realized that there was an overnight event being held for kids from the surrounding inner-city neighborhoods. He could see the pool from the lobby of the YMCA, and that was where all the action was. Children were on the deck, in the water, in long lines for the diving boards. There had to be more than 150 young people there that night.

Each of the five YMCA associations that Eric has served purposes to love, serve, and care for their cities in tangible ways that show the love of God. They want their YMCAs to be experienced by all. This value comes alive in many ways, including pool parties. This YMCA had identified kids from across the community who were in need, who may not have had the opportunity to learn to swim, and had invited them to the YMCA so they could learn how to swim and splash around with their friends.

Eric walked through the gangs of giggling kids and past sweaty teens with basketballs tucked under their arms. He greeted staff and volunteers as he moved along but made his way determinedly toward the pool deck.

Almost immediately after he walked through the doors, amid the splashing and diving and laughing, Eric spotted something that seemed off. He saw the faint outline of something at the bottom of the pool. He mentioned it to a lifeguard, who told him she'd get it after the party. She thought it was a beach towel. The small whisper in Eric's heart became a bold voice. "Get that off the bottom of the pool now!" he yelled, surprising even himself with his boldness.

The lifeguard jumped in and surfaced, not with a beach towel but with the body of a ten-year-old boy. Instantly Eric was in the water, fully clothed, swimming to meet the lifeguard halfway. He grabbed the boy and swam back to the pool deck, carrying him in his arms.

A crowd gathered. Eric shouted for everyone to stay back and for a volunteer to call 911. Heart racing, Eric flashed through his training: establish responsiveness by looking, listening, and feeling for signs of life. The boy was not breathing. His heart was not beating. Instinctively Eric grabbed the boy's shoulders and shook them, shouting, "Jimmy! Can you hear me? Jimmy!"

Even in the midst of panic and rushing adrenaline, Eric realized he had never seen this kid before and certainly did not know his name. Suddenly a teenage girl pushed through the crowd, calling, "That's my little brother! His name is Jimmy Brewster!" At this a wave of peace washed over Eric.

He had the strong sense that everything was going to be okay.

Eric began CPR right away, and in a few moments Jimmy began to cough up water. Life rushed back into his body. Soon the ambulance arrived and took him to the hospital for observation. He made a full recovery, without complications.

Jimmy is now an adult who will never forget a YMCA that was more than a gym and swim, and a leader who was willing to listen to the voice of God!

ANNIE NGWIRA

I wish Annie Ngwira and I lived a little closer to each other. She is from Zambia, and I live in Ohio. If we were closer, she would be a regular dinner guest at our house. This woman is smart, experienced, loving, and brave. She also has a fun sense of humor. While we can't have dinner very often, I get to speak with her on Zoom calls. Her internet service is usually going in and out, but her bright smile is constant.

Recently, we spoke about her history with the YMCA in Zambia. Since, as I mentioned, she is smart, experienced, loving, and funny, I'll introduce her and then just let her speak for herself.

Annie was the executive director of a YMCA in Zambia for years, and the CEO of the Zambia YMCA before that. She's traveled a lot but really loves her own home and her five dogs. She has worked in community development almost all her life, and now, during her "retirement," the government has hired her to train people in conflict resolution ahead of the national election. Here are some of her thoughts about the YMCA.

———————

When I became executive director, we already had a "Christian emphasis committee" at the YMCA. But they weren't really doing what they were supposed to be doing. They weren't doing anything uniquely Christian. So with the help of the president, who was a pastor, we worked to strengthen the committee. And that was a boost to me. Because then we could emphasize to the young people coming into our program that if they were interested, they could come for morning devotions. We didn't force anyone. But those who were willing, those who were interested, those who were curious, could join us in the morning for devotions.

Zambia is a Christian nation, but not everyone is a Christian. And most of these young people came from homes where their parents were not Christians. A number of them gave their life to Christ. They said that Jesus was transforming their lives. Most of them were very vulnerable, but after knowing who they were in Christ, they were strengthened.

Many of these young people came to the YMCA for skills training, so they could go and find employment or start a business. But by the time they received Christ, that skills training became more meaningful.

Now it wasn't just for business, but also for service. They would go out and impact the life of another person. They would go out and serve with love. And if they were going to go into business, they would do that business with the integrity and the honesty that is expected of a child of God. I was very happy and even now am very proud of them.

If you look around you, there are also many secular NGOs that are empowering young people in these fields, empowering people with knowledge and training and what have you. But as long as the central person is not changed and transformed, you find that they may finish school but aren't really productive. Maybe they go back to drugs, maybe they go back to drinking, maybe they do some other antisocial activities, and you find that their life is being wasted.

Life becomes meaningful and valuable with Christ in you, the hope of glory.

A lot of rich people in the world have achieved everything, but they still feel empty, because there's a place in each one of us reserved for the Creator Himself. And as long as He's not there, even if we say we are enjoying our lives, there is still that emptiness. So for us to be fulfilled, to live the life that we were intended to live, and to achieve the purpose for which He created us, He has to guide us. We have to know Him.

We have a lot of children who, because of the impact of HIV/AIDS in Africa, have lost parents. Because they have no one to look after them, they end up living on the streets. For them to survive on the streets, they have to live in groups. In those groups they start sniffing glue and abusing other substances that make them feel comfortable and warm. So we've developed a program for street kids.

We wanted to serve them, but we would not be another orphanage. We wanted to be a place where they could come together, have a meal, and play games, someplace where they could escape from the streets, someplace they could call "Our Place."

So we take these children off the streets and trace any surviving relative. We work to put them in a home with their relatives. From there we empower that relative and raise resources to help her take care of this child and any other children in the home, so that they don't go back to the streets.

When the kids are spending time at our center, we do devotions with them about the love of God, the love of Jesus, who Jesus Christ is. We tell them, "We love you because Jesus loves you. Jesus is our Lord and Savior, and He is also yours. He's the one who has asked us to do this project so that we can bring you here."

And that experience of being accepted, of not being looked at as a criminal, of not being looked at as the rejects of society, it warms them up. And if you sit with them and say, "What do you want to do?" they say, "I want to go back to school."

So we raised scholarship money and placed them in schools and supported them there. There were some who were much too old for school, but they said, "Take us for skills training." So we offered them skills training. Many of them are now working, managing their own lives.

———————

Annie and I talked about the great number of NGOs, or nonprofits, that there are in Africa. And we talked about why it matters that the YMCA is more than a "good works" ministry. Here is what Annie had to say.

Every NGO has a foundation. The YMCA has a foundation. If I have a vision that I want to do "ABC," I will set something up to accomplish it, to lay that foundation. But if one day I die and my children take up that organization and then change it completely, believe me, I would be complaining to Jesus and saying, "What is happening? Can you close that thing down?"

If it has lost its vision, it has lost its relevance.

The YMCA addresses three things—the triangle: the mind, the body, and the spirit. The mind is knowledge and information, mental training. The body is to be physically fit. But when George started the YMCA, he started with the spiritual man.

He started with the spiritual man and then said, "How can this be whole?" I think we should address the mind and the body, but if we remove the spiritual, then we have killed the YMCA. It is no longer the YMCA. It cannot be the YMCA. And it wouldn't have any relevance; it wouldn't have any history. I mean, it wouldn't be linked to the foundation; it would just be a strange organization.

There are millions and millions of other organizations that do not have a Christian mission. And they're operating here. This one has a Christian mission, and people want to remove the Christian mission? Just go start your own organization!

Annie said this with a big smile and a hearty laugh. But I know she was quite serious. She has seen many precious lives rescued and renewed through the powerful love of Christ in the YMCA.

JOACHIM SCHMUTZ

Joachim Schmutz is a leader in the YMCA in Germany and one of the founders, with Steve Clay, of UNIFY. UNIFY is a platform to help YMCA workers to strengthen the Christ-centered work in the YMCA, as it is expressed in the Paris Basis, and to exchange ideas about it.

Joachim started volunteering at the YMCA when he was nineteen years old, and it was there that he encountered

Jesus in a profound way. This pivoted him toward a life of service. He has been serving at the YMCA ever since.

After almost four decades in the YMCA, this humble and faithful man has the kind of insight that is a prize to grasp. I'd like to walk you through just a few of the nuggets he shared with me in our most recent conversation.

Community transformation begins with you.

At Unify we are focused on the Christian mission. But we've always thought that that begins with ourselves, in our hearts. If I am on fire for Jesus, my surroundings will change because the light of Christ shines through me. I can only be a transformer if I myself am transformed. So that's always the key focus for when YMCA workers come to Unify. If a person is able to grow in his relationship with Jesus, and his life is impacted, then he is able to impact his community.

Make space for people from all backgrounds to find Jesus.

When we meet for Unify, we want every participant to feel welcome, no matter their background. We pray for them, and then we give them space. We count on the Holy Spirit to work as we pray. Some people who come to a Unify conference may have never prayed aloud. That is okay. They can feel free not to pray. There is no pressure about anything. Usually what happens is that the Holy Spirit speaks to them, and then we get to give God the praise.

People come from all kinds of cultures and spiritual backgrounds. There may be some things that feel different from what they are used to, but we can all come together around Christ at the center. People go home from these conferences really strengthened and encouraged and ready to make an impact in their families, in their communities, and in their YMCAs.

People are drawn to Christ because of transformed lives.

In Germany, Christianity tends to have a bad image. People are turning away from the churches, and we are a very secular country. So people aren't naturally interested in becoming a Christian.

We want kids to know that Christ can make an impact in their lives and that a relationship with Jesus is a strong foundation. We want them to know that their lives can be different, that they can have eternal life. But we're not just going around saying, "Who wants to receive Jesus? Raise your hand!"

No, we play with the kids. We relate with the kids. We have fun together. We live our lives in front of them.

Eventually, naturally, the gospel becomes a part of that. Because we share our lives with them, they can read our lives even better than our words. Thankfully, our words reflect what they see in our lives. At the YMCA we have a platform to love and relate to young people. We can build relationships. We get to know them, they get to know us, and hopefully they might see a difference in our lives because we're Christians. And hopefully they might eventually open their hearts to the gospel. We go the extra mile to reach kids. We don't teach that they have to come to church to meet Jesus. We go to the kids and bring Jesus to them.

Our YMCAs are run by volunteers. The young people who come notice that all the people there serving and loving them aren't doing this for the money. This makes them think, and eventually they are more open to hearing why we are doing what we are doing, and what motivates us—and then we can share the love of Christ. Our young people appreciate that we are not just paid social workers, hired to deal with their problems, but people who really care for them.

Some of our kids have rough backgrounds and have committed crimes, or do drugs, and are in trouble with the police. We still want them to feel at home in our youth centers. As much as we can, we want to show these young people we really love them, we care for them, and that most of all we want to help them to develop good lives. And of course we can say, "Look, personally, I can share with you that I have a fulfilled life because of Christ." We don't do that all the time, but when there is an opportunity, we do. And I think the kids appreciate that.

MYITKYINA ORPHANAGE, AS TOLD BY SAM STEPHENS

In the early 2000s, as the YMCA's Asian Pacific Alliance president, Sam Stephens, visited Myanmar and spent time in the city of Myitkyina. One afternoon there still stirs in his memories, and he shared that story with me.

"This is a story of transformation. It begins with the transformation of this young man in the white shirt." Sam pointed to a picture of a tall, dark-haired, thin man in a short-sleeved white cotton button-down. The picture showed a man smiling in a sunny, pounded-dirt courtyard, surrounded by children, all standing six feet apart from one another. They were stretched out into various poses. Sam explained that this young man was teaching the kids bando, or thaing, the most popular martial art in Myanmar. The young man was an expert. He was also an ex–drug addict. He also ran this small orphanage in Myitkyina with his wife.

Sam recalled, "He was a drug addict but then had a personal encounter with Jesus, and his life was totally transformed." He had lived on the streets and knew what it was like there. Young children, both boys and girls, were exploited, trafficked, made part of the drug trade, neglected, and abused in unimaginable ways. He knew, because he had been saved out of it, so he started working with street kids.

Through his own initiative, he rented a small compound and brought kids off the streets to make a home there. He heard about the YMCA in Myanmar and wanted to see if they would help. Sam and Yip Kok Choong, the secretary general of the Asian Pacific Alliance, were visiting to check it out.

"The kids were learning discipline through martial arts, but the important thing was he had taught them to pray and to study the Word. He taught them the Word morning and evening. And the transformation that had taken place in the lives of these children was not simply because they had been rescued from the streets but because of their encounters with Jesus."

Sam showed me another picture. It was of a long table, lined with children perched along benches on either side. Only half of them were eating lunch. Half of the children were pulling warm rice from big, silver bowls and eating contentedly. The other half were sitting alongside, contentedly chatting or leaning on other children's shoulders. They were waiting for their turn to eat lunch.

The orphanage had only twenty bowls. Every day, every meal, some kids got to go first. Then the dishes would be gathered, washed, and reset so the second group could eat. Yet they all sat together each day, enjoying each other's company the whole time.

Sam asked the man about the odd setup. The young man said that he trusted God to provide for the kids and that the kids trusted him to serve them lunch each day. He could wait contentedly until God provided, and they could wait contentedly until lunch was served.

This, Sam says, is exactly the kind of initiative with which the YMCA loves to partner. The needs of others become our needs, and faith—trusting God for provision— is the centerpiece.

The YMCA did go on to partner with this little orphanage in Myitkyina, which shone its light so brightly and passed it on to many.

Sam, Annie, Joachim, Eric, and Caesar—each a beacon in the dark. There are hundreds more stories like theirs. There are hundreds more faithful YMCA servants, committed to love, compassion, truth, and action, shining around the world, ignited by Jesus, *the* light of the world.

CHAPTER 10

DIMMING LIGHT

If you have made it this far in this book, I hope you have learned something new. Maybe you've heard bits of history that surprised you, or read statements that were filed in distant memory. You may have been inspired by stories of the YMCA, old and new, from around the world.

I am not so naive, however, to think that you haven't experienced moments of restlessness. Perhaps you have the growing sense that your Y story is not quite like these Y stories, or that your experience of the mission has little resemblance to the mission of the YMCA as described on these pages.

You are not alone.

Several years ago I came across the essay "Living in the Vision of God" by Dallas Willard. He says, "The mission or missions that have been set afoot begin a subtle divergence from the vision that gripped the founder, and before too long, *the institution and its mission has become the vision*."[1]

Those words got my attention.

Willard goes on to say,

> There is a real point to saying that in religious matters
> nothing fails like success. These types of movements
> touch the human heart very deeply and serve profound
> human needs. Because of this, they soon attract many
> who do not even want the fire of the founder—they do
> not really understand it. But they do need and like the
> light and the warmth it provides. Eventually, however,
> and without consciously intending to do so, they
> extinguish the very fire that provides the light and
> warmth, or it simply dies out from lack of being tended.
> Then an operation may continue under the name,
> trading in memorabilia. But it isn't the same operation
> on the inside, and truthfully its effects are not the same.[2]

Bright lights can grow dim.

Because I love the mission of the YMCA, I have spent
years in old books studying the life cycle of mission movements. I want to understand why it is that bright lights dim.

There is a subtle and painful pattern that I have
observed within many organizations. I have studied this
pattern within churches, ministries, higher level academic
institutions and mission-driven movements like the YMCA.

Though there are certainly different components present in each life cycle, there seems to be a consistent pattern that unfolds.

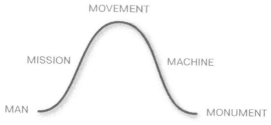

MAN

God ignites the heart of a man, a woman, or a group of people. In response to surrounding need, a holy discomfort grows within them. This restless, God-given angst combines with humility, surrender, and a desperate sense that something must be done.

MISSION

"Something must be done" becomes "this we must do." God works in surrendered dependence and clarifies a mission. Passion and heart longing become focus and action.

MOVEMENT

Results that can be attributed only to God have an amazing impact upon the community. The mission multiplies. Lives are changed. The heart of the mission and the strategy is replicated. Buildings, budgets, programs, and infrastructure are put in place to support the mission and the movement.

The light shines brightly.

MACHINE

Mostly unnoticed, there is a drift in purpose. Results, programs, and sustaining buildings gradually become the mission. The humble posture of dependence, surrender, and seeking God as the source of vision is incrementally replaced by the pride of accomplishment. The original vision is transformed into nothing more than the goal of maintaining results.

MONUMENT

Aim has completely drifted from the original mission and from its empowering source. The fire is out. What was once alive, organic, and aflame feels dead, still, and cold. Although a monument may stand, even for centuries, it no longer has an impact on the world around it.

I believe it is crucial to reflect on this pattern. Learn to see each of these stages. Consider where your YMCA is on the curve.

John Mott once reflected on how it would be that the YMCA could remain spiritually vital and fruitful amid a world that is ever changing. He held up the YMCA's great aim. He stood upon the YMCA's foundation. And as the president of the World Alliance, he spoke a bold word to the fourteen thousand YMCAs that would one day encompass the world.

How can a YMCA stay spiritually vital and fruitful?

> *The Association must steadfastly resist the danger of becoming a mere human institution—in a general sense religious but not emphatically, pervasively, and contagiously Christian. This essential must never be compromised, obscured, or abandoned for the sake of any plausible outward success or worldly advantage, for such a course would mark the beginning of the end. Wherever an Association lacks world-conquering power, it is because it has to some extent been conquered by the world.*[3]

Just twenty years later Paul Limbert raised the same warning.

> *It is easy to see the dangers and limitations of this wide range of activities that is so characteristic of YMCAs. Leaders may get so preoccupied in promoting and directing these activities that they lose sight of the Christian purpose that first inspired the program. The YMCA tends to become a large-scale business enterprise in which economic considerations outweigh religious convictions.... Theodore Roosevelt once said, "The thing I like about you YMCA folks is the way*

you mix religion and common sense." But all too often
the religious element is so diluted that the result is a
very thin mixture.[4]

If John Mott was, essentially, reflecting on the implications of this bell curve in 1926, and Paul Limbert was again in 1944, it seems imperative that we join them in the same kind of evaluation today.

Let me step outside of this somewhat academic reasoning for a moment and offer some encouragement. If I did not believe that our foundation was still strong, if I did not believe that our mission still stands, if I were not convinced that the fire that lit George Williams's heart can still blaze, I would never have taken your time with this book.

The light from this flame can still shine today.
However, sometimes a flame simply needs to be kindled.

CHAPTER 11
REKINDLED LIGHT

I told you that my family is building a farmhouse in the woods. What we have learned this past year, beyond great patience, is that before a foundation is laid and a house is built, land must be cleared. Clearing land in the woods means lots of fires. My boys and I have been cutting down trees with chain saws and hauling wood away to burn. We've spent nights on camp chairs, warmed and fascinated by the beauty of the flames.

Some of these fires have burned so hot that even a few days later a tiny stream of smoke is wafting up from the ashes. This is when my wife takes over. I don't know where she learned it, but she has an uncanny ability to stir up the ashes, add fresh wood, blow the right amount of oxygen into the embers, and before you know it, the dwindling flames are alive and dancing once more.

> From the ashes a fire shall be woken,
> A light from the shadows shall spring.[1]

We've just spent a chapter talking about dimming light. Perhaps you will sigh and say, "Those stories of the light and mission of the YMCA are great, but I have to get back to my real job in my real YMCA. How do those idealistic mission thoughts impact my world?"

I won't waste your time with a formula for relighting the beacon of your YMCA. It's never a simple or easy process.

But just as my wife has a mysterious way of stirring up ashes, adding fresh wood, and blowing the right amount of oxygen, there are themes of the movement that seem to relight mission fires. The themes I have observed are a commitment to pray, to care, to depend, and to remember.

COMMIT TO PRAY

Jeremiah Lanphier was a young businessman who lived in mid-nineteenth-century New York City. He was an earnest young man who was determined to live a missional life; in the language of today's YMCA, he wanted to be a change agent and live for a greater story.

His local church appointed him to be a city missionary. Lanphier didn't charge out and execute a list of to-dos. He didn't try to make change happen now. Instead, helpless and overwhelmed at the scope of the task, he set out to walk the streets of New York City. He wanted to serve people. He wanted to reach people. But he didn't know what to do.

Every day at noon he found himself exhausted. He made a habit of slipping into a little room at the back of a church on Fulton Street to pray, asking God for strength for the remainder of the day.

One day something changed. On September 23, 1857, Jeremiah prayed a simple prayer. He looked to God with a yearning heart and open hands and prayed, "Lord, what would you have me do?"

As he waited and listened, he felt in his spirit a gentle stirring to start a prayer meeting. He prayed, and the Lord told him to pray some more.

Believing he had heard from God, he said, "I'll do it," and quickly purposed to host a prayer meeting every Wednesday from 12:00 p.m. to 1:00 p.m. For almost a year the YMCA had been hosting noon prayer meetings at the Dutch church on Fulton Street. They were well attended for a few months but had not really caught on. Nearly a year after they began, the church was almost empty at the noon hour.

Jeremiah approached the YMCA leadership, asking for help to restart the prayer meetings. He passed out invitations, hung flyers, and anticipated a great turnout as he followed the prompting he'd heard from the Lord.

Wednesday arrived. The first prayer meeting began. Lanphier was all alone in the church. So from 12:00 to 12:30, he sought the Lord by himself. At 12:30 two people walked in. A half hour later a few more showed up. By the end of the meeting, six people had gathered for prayer.

In the second week, twenty people showed up. The third week, forty people showed up.

God had his hand on these simple prayer meetings. He was answering Jeremiah's simple prayer. What happened next could only have been inspired by God.

Within six months there were ten thousand people meeting to pray in more than 150 prayer meetings all over New York City. The YMCA network responded to what the Holy Spirit was doing by organizing and leading more prayer meetings. A movement had been ignited!

Through the network of the YMCA, this movement spread to other cities. A young person went back to his hometown, Philadelphia, and with several of his YMCA friends began a prayer meeting. Before long the YMCA was sponsoring noon prayer meetings in every church and firehouse in the city.

The Baltimore association hosted five prayer meetings in the morning and four later in the day. Two thousand people a day attended the Cleveland association prayer meetings. A revival was sweeping the country through YMCA prayer meetings!

The greatest revival America has ever experienced happened through people who gathered together to pray, and the YMCA play an amazing role.

This story is dramatic and far-reaching, but I am inspired that it began with an overwhelmed young man who prayed a simple prayer: "Lord, what would you have me do?"

I have studied nearly every significant moment in the history of the YMCA. I have looked through thousands of books and heard the stories of countless leaders. Over and over again I have observed that prayer is embedded in almost every important moment in this movement.

The story of the YMCA began when a depleted, exhausted young man did not know what to do. He did not know what to do, so he prayed. He prayed, name by name, for his fellow factory workers.

The YMCA movement was ignited when a group of young men got on their knees on a dorm room floor to pray for their workplace, their boss, and their coworkers.

The story of the YMCA began to encompass the world when one hundred young people got on their knees and prayed all night that God would use them to shine the light of Jesus all across the globe.

The story of the YMCA was born not two hundred years ago but two thousand years ago, when the founder of the YMCA, Jesus, lifted his head to heaven and prayed for us to find unity in Him.

———————

The YMCA has always been a movement tethered to prayer.

If you are thinking, "I want to be a part of the shining light. What should I do?" You already know the answer. Pray.

Are you leading a local YMCA? Start off the morning by closing your office door, lifting your heart to God, and dedicating your day to him in prayer.

Do you have employees who report to you? Pray for them name by name.

Do you coach a team at your YMCA? Pray for your kids.

Do you feel that your YMCA has drifted from its aim? In the quietness of your heart, boldly pray, "Your kingdom come, Your will be done, in this YMCA as it is in heaven."

If you really want to see a bold move of God, gather a few people with you, pick a day, and start a little prayer meeting at noon. Crazy things have been known to happen in the movement of the YMCA when people pray.

———————

George Williams had a good friend by the name of Charles Spurgeon, who was the long-serving pastor of the Metropolitan Tabernacle in London. One day a few young men were taking a tour of the massive building, whose congregation dated back to the early seventeenth century.[2]

They had no idea that their tour guide was Spurgeon himself. As the story goes, he told the group that he would show them the sanctuary and the pulpit, but first he wanted to show them how it was possible to heat a church that large.

They headed down flights of stairs, entered the basement, and opened a door. Inside, from wall to wall, were people together on their knees in prayer.

The old pastor looked at the young men and said, "Here is the powerhouse of this church."[3]

Prayer is the powerhouse—the fire—that heats our movement.

If the YMCA is going to shine like fourteen thousand lighthouses, the burning center is prayer.

COMMIT TO CARE

In 2018 YMCA leaders from around the world gathered for the World Alliance meetings in Chiang Mai, Thailand. We quickly realized that the entire world was watching Chiang Mai that week, and it had nothing at all to do with us.

Just north of Chiang Mai, in the Tham Luang cave, the Wild Boars, a football team of twelve young boys and their coach, were trapped in a cave. The team had gone exploring, deep into dark caverns, when heavy rainfall flash flooded the cave. Having climbed to higher ground to escape the waters, the team was trapped.

As the water rose, their lights began to dim, along with their hopes. They knew the water would eventually overtake them, and there was no escape.

While they couldn't get out, divers could get in. And in they went. Equipped with oxygen tanks, light, and fresh hope, teams of divers navigated the treacherous cave, delivering precious oxygen to the boys in the cave.

Over the next two weeks, hundreds of people: divers, medical personnel, engineers, and soldiers, worked together to pump water out of the cave, to bring the team resources, and finally to get them out.

The world watched and cheered.

We YMCA leaders were glued to the news and were amazed by the unfolding story. At one point we tried to go to the caves to offer help and prayer, but the roads were blocked.

Looking back, it seems an apt metaphor for who we are and what we are meant to be. The YMCA is not afraid of dark places. We are going in!

We kneel beside dying soldiers on the battlefield, we run orphanages in impoverished lands, and we don't back away from the darkness in our own communities.

There are few places darker than a prisoner of war camp. The German theologian Jürgen Moltmann knew that well. After being drafted into the Nazi army as an eighteen-year-old, he barely survived bombings, surrendered to the first British soldier he saw, and then spent three years in prison camps in Scotland, Belgium, and England. The horror of prison camp, combined with the guilt of what he had been involved with, led him to a place of deep soul-darkness.

A prison camp chaplain gave him a New Testament. Moltmann began to read God's Word. He read that God loved him and was present with him, even in a prison camp.

Later he was transferred to an educational camp in England, called Norton Camp. It was run by the YMCA.

When German prisoners arrived, they were welcomed with genuine kindness, offered homemade food, and treated with holistic care. This is the stunning kind of care that loves enemies. It is the care that crosses the road to tend to the wounds of "those people." This is care that transforms. It is the radical kind of love to which Jesus calls his followers.

Moltmann had been imprisoned for three years, but there he found freedom. In the midst of great darkness, he was made alive with hope. When the YMCA cared, even for "the enemy," transformation was unleashed.[4]

The YMCA can still be a movement that cares!

There are many health clubs in the world. We have a buffet of opportunities to pay a monthly fee, tone our body, stretch in a yoga class, and sign up our kids for youth basket-ball. There are thousands of childcare centers. There are plenty of camps.

The YMCA is meant to be so much more. If you are part of a YMCA and something in you longs for a brighter fire, what should you do?

Assess your community. Look for a need. Pray. Go after a cause. Find the dark places. See who needs help. Pray. Look for the unnoticed person who longs to be significant. Pray. Love a kid and speak hope to them.

You may have to start alone, but if you pray and if you care, you won't be alone for long. As a parent of four young men, I can say with authority that the next generation longs to be a part of something great. They want their lives to be swept into a story that is bigger than themselves, one that brings meaning to others' lives. If you want to build a house for a homeless family, *they will help*. If there is a great service opportunity, across the ocean or across the road, *they will go!*

But friends, if your highest vision is to be a family friendlier version of the health club down the street, honestly, *they won't care.*

There's no need to advertise that you care. Just begin. (And pray.)

I've heard that Dwight L. Moody once said, "We are told to let our light shine, and if it does, we won't need to tell anybody it does. Lighthouses don't fire cannons to call attention to their shining—they just shine."

COMMIT TO DEPEND (ON GOD)

My favorite phrase on the pillar in St. Paul's courtyard is the phrase "inspired of God."

"Inspire comes from the Latin word that means to inflame or to blow into. When you inspire something it is as if you are blowing air over a low flame to make it grow."[5]

Twelve young men gathered together in a tiny dorm room, prayerful and God-inspired to care for their fellow men. Only God could blow upon that spark and grow a movement.

One retired sea captain, walking the fishing docks of Boston, prayerful and God-inspired to care for weary sailors. Only God could blow upon that spark and grow a movement.

One woman in Zambia, passionate but under-resourced, prayerful and God-inspired to care for the impoverished. Only God could blow upon that spark and grow a movement.

One street kid in Myanmar who grew up, met Jesus, and with his twenty bowls decided he wanted to house, feed, teach, and love kids just as he had been. Only God could blow upon that spark and grow a movement.

The YMCA has never found its strength in impressive strategies or perfectly executed quarterly goals. The YMCA has thrived when men and women depend on God to do what only He can do. Its greatest leaders have been known for their humility and dependence on God.

Dwight L. Moody had a fourth-grade education. He was criticized for his poor grammar and would sometimes stumble over challenging words when he read the Bible. (When he did, he asked for help: the mark of a humble man.) Despite all this, night after night tens of thousands would fill great halls to listen to him preach.[6]

D. L. Moody believed that his strength was in his weakness.

"While in England he heard evangelist Henry Varley say, 'The world has yet to see what God can do through a man who is totally yielded to Him.' Moody was captivated by these words and resolved, 'By the Grace of God, I will be that man!'"[7]

He was humble and dependent.

Oswald Chambers rarely had an impressive plan in place. He didn't intend to write one of the most famous devotional books in the history of Christianity or to be a household name. He was simply dependent on God to show him each step in the path of his life, and he had a quiet trust that God would write the story that he wanted in his life.

He wrote this to his parents:

My dear Mother and Father,

Florence will have told you of my decision to offer for the front as a chaplain, for "first aid" spiritually. I wanted you to know as soon as I did myself. Nothing is arranged or even clear by any means yet, nothing but my decision before the Lord. I shall do my human best naturally, but as in many times in the past, I shall find God opening up the way. My mind is clear regarding God's call, the rest will "fall out" or "in" as He ordains....

I have a strong impression that the YMCA hut will be the plan adopted, but I do not know. However, He knows and I know He knows, and I know that I'll never think of anything He will forget, so I just go steadily on as I have always done, and He will engineer the circumstances.

Oswald is known for this counsel: "Trust God and do the next thing."[8]

The YMCA is not built on the backs of the smartest, the wealthiest, the most savvy, or even the wisest. As much as the YMCA has succeeded in its mission, it has been because of those who were the most humble, the most dependent.

This is good news! The pressure is off. You don't need to be anyone other than yourself. You don't need to be better. The story of the YMCA is the story of the gospel; it's all about who you trust.

I am regularly grateful for this truth.

COMMIT TO REMEMBER

There is a Bible verse which is, in my opinion, the most discouraging verse in the Bible. But before we get there, let me point you to a joyful verse, which is full of life and hope:

> Israel served the Lord all the days of Joshua, and all the days of the elders who outlived Joshua and had known all the work that the Lord did for Israel.
>
> —Joshua 24:31 ESV

The people of God experienced the presence of God. They lived within His story. They knew Him and all of His work. His stories were told and His work was known.

I wish I could stop there. I wish that verse could be said of every following generation. But unfortunately, if you flip just one or two pages to the right, you will come across the most discouraging verse in the Bible:

After that whole generation had been gathered to their ancestors, another generation grew up who knew neither the LORD *NOR WHAT HE HAD DONE FOR* ISRAEL.

—Judges 2:10 NIV

The next generation *did not know*. They didn't know the Lord or the work He had done. They didn't know their own story!

How can this be?

I think the explanation is pretty simple: the previous generation forgot to tell. They never passed down their story.

The generation that saw Jericho's walls fall down, the generation that entered the promised land, the generation that knew the Lord and experienced His story, dropped the baton when it came to passing it down to the next generation.

There are some commands in the Bible that thread the story from Genesis to Revelation. They appear so often that they must be central to the heart of God. One of these commands is the command, "Remember!" Open any book of the

Bible, and there is a good chance that you will bump into this command. In every major transition point in the story of God, He calls His people to remember. During the Old Testament feasts and festivals, there was usually a leader who would stand up among the people and say, "Remember our story! Remember who we are! Remember we were once slaves in Egypt, but God sent a Redeemer. Remember that we wandered in the desert, but God brought us to the promised land. Remember that we were at war against the Philistines and Goliath, but God raised up a Rescuer. Remember. Remember. Remember!"

Why is it so central to the heart of God that we remember?

I believe that when we remember what God has done, our faith is strengthened and we believe what God can do! The story of our past propels the story of our future.

I write this next statement carefully and with much pain in my heart. When it comes to the story of the YMCA, I believe many in this movement are in a Judges 2:10 moment.

Generations experienced the bright shining light of this mission. They knew the Lord and His work. But those generations failed to pass it down. They didn't tell. They forgot their story.

It's been said that those who forget their history are bound to repeat it. May the YMCA remember our history, so we may indeed repeat it!

We must make it known. We must not be silent. We must remember.

Do you want to rekindle the fire that once burned bright and clear? Don't just shelve this book and forget the stories. Let them be known. Share a story with your kids. Begin a staff meeting with, "Has anyone heard the name George Williams?"

———————————

Pray. Care. Cultivate a humble dependence on God. Remember the work of God and look for ways to tell His story.

These are not formulaic steps but attitudes of the heart.

When God looks upon a humble, praying, caring, remembering heart totally yielded to Himself, He has a way of saying, "That's what I'm looking for! Now watch what I can do."

CHAPTER 12

DO IT AGAIN

Five young men met in a hayfield in a small town in Massachusetts. Sam Mills, a student at Williams College, had called his classmates together to commit their lives to a great mission. In 1805, the Great Awakening was rippling across the country and these men were moved with a longing for something more in their lives. They wanted their stories to be part of God's story, so they met to pray and talk about what they must do.

Caught up in fervent conversation, they didn't notice that the sky above them had turned a deep shade of purple-black and that the temperature had dropped dramatically. Bits of hay were flying through the air, and with a flash of lightning, a huge storm was upon them.

Seeing no other shelter, they dove into a haystack and continued their prayer meeting. The Spirit of God met them in that haystack, and their passion formed into the aim of their lives. They committed their lives to sharing the good news of Jesus with the world.

"Finally after singing a hymn, Mills looked at the others, and over the roar of the drenching rain, and with flashes of lightning reflecting in his eyes, cried out, 'We can do this, if we will!' Something broke loose in that moment within the hearts of all five. All pointed back to that moment as the one that changed them forever."[1]

A few years after the boys prayed in the hay, some women bought the field for a dollar and built a monument in honor of the Haystack Prayer Meeting.

While none of those wet, hay-covered boys could have predicted it, this moment of conviction, earnestness, passion, willingness, and prayer became the foundation for mission work that continues today across the world. InterVarsity traces its formative spark back to this moment, along with the Student Volunteer Movement and the YMCA.

It's amazing how much of the YMCA story has to do with wet hay, sudden storms, and bold prayer meetings!

In 1877, nearly seventy years after the Haystack Revival, Luther Wishard became the first full-time employee of the YMCA of the USA. I'm sure he was a little overwhelmed.

He couldn't have known what to do or how to lead this movement.

But like so many of the leaders who have shaped this movement, he began with prayer. In humble dependence on God, and the faith that God could use the YMCA, he prayed that the YMCA would shine the light of Christ around the world.

Wishard wanted to dedicate his work with the YMCA to the Lord. He wanted to mark that moment in his memory forever. So he took a trip to Williamstown, Massachusetts, and found the Haystack Revival marker.

Luther Wishard got down on his knees in front of the monument and prayed this prayer: "Lord, do it again! Where water once flowed, let it flow again."[2]

He went on. "I am willing to go anywhere at any time to do anything for Jesus."[3]

What a beautiful prayer. It is a prayer of boldness: "Do what only you can do, God." And, "You have done it before. Do it again!" It is a prayer of surrender: "Anywhere, anytime, anything for Jesus. I am yours, God."

I love the YMCA. I love its story and its people. I love the bold mission that has stood strong for nearly two centuries. I am inspired by its founder, George Williams, a relatively unknown man used by God to light a mighty beacon.

Like George Williams, like the Haystack five, like Luther Wishard, I too have a longing. I believe it is a God-given longing. It keeps me up at night and brings me hopeful tears. My longing, my prayer, is that one day this movement will be known not for a song and not for its gym but for its light. I pray that YMCA leaders would remember their target and adjust their aim. I long for communities in darkness to be transformed by the light of Jesus Christ.

Lord, let fourteen thousand lighthouses shine again!

A few years ago I took a trip to Williamstown, Massachusetts, and found the field where the Haystack marker stands. The sun was just rising when I got to the field. I knelt on the damp ground in the same place where Luther Wishard had. My eyes filled with tears, and I lifted my hands to the Lord. In that sacred moment I whispered a prayer.

"Lord, do it again! Where water once flowed, let it flow again. I am willing to go anywhere, anytime, and do anything for Jesus."

I lingered there in the early sun for a moment and then stood up, wiped the tears from my eyes and the dirt from my knees, and walked away, forever committed to shine.

Would you pray this with me?

Will you care with me, depend with me, and remember with me?

And then will you pray again?

If we will, fourteen thousand lighthouses will light up the world.

ROBERT GIBSON

APPENDIX

CHALLENGE 21

1998
Freschen, Germany
14th World Council

Affirming the Paris Basis adopted in 1855 as the ongoing foundation statement of the mission of the YMCA, at the threshold of the third millennium we declare that the YMCA is a world-wide Christian, ecumenical, voluntary movement for women and men with special emphasis on and the genuine involvement of young people and that it seeks to share the Christian ideal of building a human community of justice with love, peace and reconciliation for the fullness of life for all creation.

Each member YMCA is therefore called to focus on certain challenges which will be prioritized according to its own context. These challenges, which are an evolution of the Kampala Principles, are:

- Sharing the good news of Jesus Christ and striving for spiritual, intellectual and physical well-being of individuals and wholeness of communities.

- Empowering all, especially young people and women to take increased responsibilities and assume leadership at all levels and working towards an equitable society.

- Advocating for and promoting the rights of women and upholding the rights of children.

- Fostering dialogue and partnership between people of different faiths and ideologies and recognizing the cultural identities of people and promoting cultural renewal.

- Committing to work in solidarity with the poor, dispossessed, uprooted people and oppressed racial, religious and ethnic minorities.

- Seeking to be mediators and reconcilers in situations of conflict and working for meaningful participation and advancement of people for their own self-determination.

- Defending God's creation against all that would destroy it and preserving and protecting the earth's resources for coming generations. To face these challenges, the YMCA will develop patterns of cooperation at all levels that enable self-sustenance and self-determinationı.

THE KAMPALA PRINCIPLES

July 1973
Kampala, Uganda
6th World Council

The Paris Basis expresses that Christ is the center of the Movement, which is conceived as a world-wide fellowship uniting Christians of all confessions. It is consistent with an open membership policy, involving people irrespective of faith as well as age, sex, race and social condition. The Basis is not designed to serve as a condition of individual YMCA membership, which is deliberately left to the discretion of constituent movements of the World Alliance. The Basis makes clear that the constituent movements of the Alliance have full freedom to express their purpose in other terms designed to correspond more directly to the needs and aspirations of those whom they are seeking to serve, provided these are regarded by the World Alliance as being consistent with the Paris Basis. Recognising the character of the YMCAs in the world today, this act of acknowledging the Paris Basis places upon the various associations and their members as fellow workers with God such imperatives as:

1. To work for equal opportunity and justice for all.

2. To work for and maintain an environment in which relationships among people are characterized by love and understanding.

3. To work for and maintain conditions, within the YMCA and in society, its organizations and institutions, which allow for honesty, depth and creativity.

4. To develop and maintain leadership and program patterns which exemplify the varieties and depth of Christian experience.

5. To work for the development of the whole person.[2]

NOTES

FORWARD

INTRODUCTION

J. E. Hodder Williams, *The Life of Sir George Williams*
(Cincinnati: Jennings and Graham, 1906), 275.
[2] Clarence Prouty Shedd, *History of the World's Alliance of Young Men's Christian Associations*, 1st ed.
(London: S.P.C.K. for the World's Committee of Young Men's Christian Associations, 1955), 364.

PART 1: THE MAN

CHAPTER 1: THE PATH

J. E. Hodder Williams, *The Life of Sir George Williams*
(Cincinnati: Jennings and Graham, 1906), 6–9.

[2] Ibid., 15.

[3] Ibid., 14.

[4] Mo Willems, *Goldilocks and the Three Dinosaurs*
(New York: Balzer + Bray, 2012).

CHAPTER 2: ONWARD AND OUTWARD

J. E. Hodder Williams, *The Life of Sir George Williams*
(Cincinnati: Jennings and Graham, 1906), 21.

[2] Frederick Engels, *The Condition of the Working-Class in England in 1844 with a Preface Written in 1892*, version 17306 (The Project Gutenberg, 2005), www.gutenberg.org/files/17306/17306-h/17306-h.htm, 163–65.

[3] L. L. Doggett, *History of the Young Men's Christian Association*, vol. 1
(Cleveland: Imperial Press, 1896), 31.

4 Williams, *The Life of Sir George Williams*, 25.

5 Ibid., 26–27.

6 Ibid.

7 Ibid.

8 Ibid.

9 Ibid., 46.

10 Ibid.

11 Doggett, *History of the Young Men's Christian Association*, 33.

12 J. E. Hodder Williams, *The Father of the Red Triangle: The Life of Sir George Williams, Founder of the Y.M.C.A.* (London: Hodder and Stoughton, 1918), 40.

13 Williams, *The Life of Sir George Williams*, 49.

14 Doggett, *History of the Young Men's Christian Association*, 33.

15 Williams, *The Life of Sir George Williams*, 95.

15 Doggett, *History of the Young Men's Christian Association*, 48.

16 Ibid., 97.

17 Doggett, *History of the Young Men's Christian Association*, 36

18 Ibid.

19 Williams, *The Life of Sir George Williams*, 50.

20 Ibid., 106.

21 G. W. Wilson and Co., Blackfriars Bridge, 188_, Library of Congress (Library of Congress Prints and Photographs Division Washington, D.C., 20540 USA), www.loc.gov/resource/ppmsca.06814/.

22 Doggett, *History of the Young Men's Christian Association*, 38.

23 Ibid., 39.

24 Ibid.

25 Williams, *The Life of Sir George Williams*, 107.

26 Ibid., 111.

27 Doggett, *History of the Young Men's Christian Association*, 40.

28 Williams, *The Life of Sir George Williams*, 111.

29 J. E. Hodder Williams, (Cincinnati: Jennings and Graham, 1906), 113.

CHAPTER 3: FINISHING WELL

J. E. Hodder Williams, *The Father of the Red Triangle: The Life of Sir George Williams, Founder of the Y.M.C.A.* (London: Hodder and Stoughton, 1918).

[2] Ibid., 244.

[3] J. E. Hodder Williams, *The Life of Sir George Williams* (Cincinnati: Jennings and Graham, 1906), 243.

[4] J. C. G. Binfield, *That Dear Man, George Williams, 1821–1905* (London: National Council of the YMCAs of England and Wales, 1970), 1.

[5] Ibid.

[6] Williams, *The Life of Sir George Williams,* 217.

[7] Williams, *The Father of the Red Triangle,* 86.

[8] Ibid., 87.

[9] Williams, *The Life of Sir George Williams,* 158.

[10] L. L. Doggett, *History of the Young Men's Christian Association,* vol. 1 (Cleveland: Imperial Press, 1896), 51.

[11] Williams, *The Life of Sir George Williams,* 87–88.

[12] Ibid., 178.

[13] Ibid., 86.

[14] Ibid., 217.

[15] Doggett, *History of the Young Men's Christian Association,* 48.

[16] Ibid., 51.

[17] Williams, *The Father of the Red Triangle,* 256–57.

[18] "Plaque: YMCA," London Remembers, www.londonremembers.com/memorials/ymca.

PART 2: THE MISSION

In 1855 delegates throughout the world gathered together in Paris, France, to establish the mission statement of the YMCA. This statement continues to be the global purpose of the movement. Individual countries have the freedom to contextualize these words to meet the needs of their service area; however, each country pledges its commitment to this great statement. "Paris Basis—1855," YMCA International—World Alliance of YMCAs, World YMCA (September 19, 2020), www.ymca.int/about-us/ymca-history/paris-basis-1855/.

CHAPTER 4: THE AIM

www.tampabay.com/archive/2004/08/23/americans-pick-wrong-time-to-be-off-target/#.

[2] J. R. R. Tolkien, *The Fellowship of the Ring: Being the First Part of The Lord of the Rings* (New York: Del Rey, 2012), 278.

CHAPTER 5: BEGINNINGS

Charles Howard Hopkins, *History of the Y.M.C.A. in North America* (New York: Association Press, 1951), 5.

[2] "YMCA History," YMCA International—World Alliance of YMCAs, World YMCA (September 19, 2020), www.ymca.int/about-us/ymca-history/.

[3] Tom Welch, "Thomas Sullivan—Founder of the 1st YMCA in the United States," YMCA Spiritual Legacy Series (Central Florida YMCA).

[4] Ibid.

[5] Hans J. Hillerbrand, *The Encyclopedia of Protestantism*, vol. 4 (New York: Routledge, 2004), 869.

[6] Hopkins, *History of the YMCA in North America*, 18.

[7] Ibid.

[8] J. E. Hodder Williams, *The Life of Sir George Williams* (1906; repr., Freedonia Press, 2002), 180–81.

[9] John R. Mott, *Confronting Young Men with the Living Christ* (New York: Association Press, 1923), 14.

CHAPTER 6: FOUNDATIONS

Clarence Prouty Shedd, *History of the World's Alliance of Young Men's Christian Associations*, 1st ed. (London: S.P.C.K. for the World's Committee of Young Men's Christian Associations, 1955), x.

[2] "Paris Basis—1855," YMCA International—World Alliance of YMCAs, World YMCA (September 19, 2020), www.ymca.int/about-us/ymca-history/paris-basis-1855/.

[3] C. S. Lewis, *Mere Christianity,* rev. ed. (London: William Collins, 2017), 55–56.

[4] Ulrich Parzany, "III. The Whole World: The Uniqueness of Christ II," Lausanne Movement (October 19, 2018), https://lausanne.org/content/manila-1989-documents.

[5] Shedd, *History of the World's Alliance of Young Men's Christian Associations*, 517.

[6] Paul M. Limbert, *New Perspectives for the YMCA* (Association Press, 1964), 58.

[7] Oswald Chambers, *He Shall Glorify Me: Talks on the Holy Spirit and Other Themes* (London: Oswald Chambers Publications Association and Christian Literature Crusade, 1975), 139.

[8] Oswald Chambers and James Reimann, *My Utmost for His Highest: Selections for Every Day* (Grand Rapids: Discovery House, 1995), November 29.

[9] Dwight Lyman Moody, *Pleasure and Profit in Bible Study* (New York: Fleming H. Revell, 1895), 8.

[10] Caesar Molebatsi, "Reaching the Oppressed," *Transformation: An International Journal of Holistic Mission Studies* 7, no. 1 (1990): 25–27, https://doi.org/10.1177/026537889000700110.

[11] Martin Luther King, "The Christian Pertinence of Eschatological Hope," The Martin Luther King, Jr., Research and Education Institute, Howard Gotlieb Archival Research Center (February 15, 1950).

[12] Andrew Murray, *Waiting on God: Daily Messages for a Month* (Nabu Press, 2010), day 8.

[13] A. W. Tozer, *The Pursuit of God: The Human Thirst for the Divine* (Chicago: Moody Publishers, 2015), 90.

CHAPTER 7: BUILDING WELL

Paul M. Limbert, *New Perspectives for the YMCA* (Association Press, 1964), 21.

2 Lyle W. Dorsett, *A Passion for Souls: The Life of D. L. Moody* (Chicago: Moody Publishers, 2003), 85.

3 R. A. Torrery, *Why God Used D. L. Moody* (New York: Fleming H. Revel, 1923), 46.

4 Dorsett, *A Passion for Souls*, 73.

5 Ibid.

6 "The Funeral of Reverend Anthony Bowen," *Evening Star* (July 24, 1871), https://chroniclingamerica.loc.gov/lccn/sn83045462/1871-07-24/ed-1/seq-4/.

7 Ella V. Moran, "Anthony Bowen," *Negro History Bulletin* 8, no. 1 (1944): 5–21, www.jstor.org/stable/44214310.

8 Ibid.

9 "The Funeral of Reverend Anthony Bowen."

10 Dave McCasland, *Oswald Chambers: Abandoned to God; The Life Story of the Author of My Utmost for His Highest* (Grand Rapids: Discovery House, 1993), 237.

11 Ibid., 220.

12 "The Nobel Peace Prize 1946," NobelPrize.org (2021), www.nobelprize.org/prizes/peace/1946/summary/.

13 Frederick W. Haberman, "Nobel Lectures in Peace 1926–1950," *Nobel Lectures, 1926–1950* (World Scientific, 1999), 1946, https://doi.org/10.1142/3740.

14 C. Howard Hopkins, "The Legacy of John R. Mott," *International Bulletin of Missionary Research* 5, no. 2 (1981): 70–73, https://doi.org/10.1177/239693938100500205.

15 www.thetravelingteam.org/articles/john-r-mott-letters.

16 Basil Joseph Matthews, *John R. Mott, World Citizen* (New York: Harper, 1934), 44.

17 George Irving, "The Beginnings of Great Things," *North American Student* (October 1916), 66.

18 https://christianhistoryinstitute.org/magazine/article/missions-and-ecumenism-mott.

[19] Houghton, Graham; Paul, K.T. https://www.encyclopedia.com/international/encyclopedias-almanacs-transcripts-and-maps/paul-k-t.

[20] "The Young Men of India" (1895), Kautz Family YMCA Archives, https://archives.lib.umn.edu/repositories/7/archival_objects/227467.

[21] Geneva YMCA, "Tribute to Henry Dunant: Founding Member of the World Alliance of YMCAs," *YMCA World* 4 (2010): 6.

[22] Donald McCuaig, "James Naismith: Inventor of Basketball," *YMCA World* 4 (December 2010): 9.

[23] Tom Welch, "James Naismith—Inventor of Basketball," YMCA Spiritual Legacy Series (Central Florida YMCA).

[24] Emmett Dedmon, *Great Enterprises: 100 Years of the YMCA of Metropolitan Chicago* (New York: Rand McNally, 1957), 62.

[25] Ibid., 79.

[26] Birmingham Family YMCA, *Brick by Brick: Rebuilding Christian Emphasis in Your YMCA* (Birmingham, AL: Birmingham Family YMCA, 1992), 8–9.

[27] Ibid., 10.

[28] https://archives.lib.umn.edu/repositories/7/resources/958; www.ymca.int/member/ymca-in-latin-america-and-caribbean/ymca-brazil/; https://archives.lib.umn.edu/repositories/7/resources/959; www.njymca-ywca.org/en/about.php?cid=13.

CHAPTER 8: CHRISTIAN PRINCIPLES

YMCA of the USA, unpublished internal document, Chicago, n.d.

[2] Young Men's Christian Association, *Fifty Year's Work amongst Young Men in All Lands: A Review of the Work of the Young Men's Christian Associations* (London: Exeter Hall—Botolph Printing Works, 1894), viii, ix.

PART 3: THE MOVEMENT

CHAPTER 9: SPREADING LIGHT

The Lord of the Rings: The Return of the King, directed by Peter Jackson (Burbank, CA: New Line Cinema, 2003).

2 "Plaque: YMCA," London Remembers, www.londonremembers.com/memorials/ymca.

CHAPTER 10: DIMMING LIGHT

Dallas Willard, "Living in the Vision of God," https://dwillard.org/articles/living-in-the-vision-of-god.

2 Ibid.

3 John Raleigh Mott, *Confronting Young Men with the Living Christ* (London: Hodder and Stoughton, 1926).

4 Paul Limbert, *Christian Emphasis in YMCA Program* (New York: Association Press, 1944), 14.

CHAPTER 11: REKINDLED LIGHT

J. R. R. Tolkien., *The Fellowship of the Ring: Being the First Part of The Lord of the Rings* (New York: Del Rey, 2012), 278.

2 "Metropolitan Tabernacle," Charles Haddon Spurgeon's Tabernacle—Metropolitan Tabernacle, www.metropolitantabernacle.org/church-details/history.

3 Lewis A. Drummond, "The Secrets of Spurgeon's Preaching: Christian History Magazine," Christian History Institute (1991), https://christianhistoryinstitute.org/magazine/article/secrets-of-spurgeon.

4 Philip Yancey, "God Behind Barbed Wire," *Christianity Today* (August 29, 2005), www.christianitytoday.com/ct/2005/september/20.120.html.

5 "Inspire—Dictionary Definition," Vocabulary.com, www.vocabulary.com/dictionary/inspire.

6 Erwin W. Lutzer, "Totally Yielded to God," Moody Church Media (2014), www.moodymedia.org/articles/moody-man-our-times/.

7 Ibid.

8 Oswald Chambers and James Reimann, *My Utmost for His Highest: Selections for Every Day* (Grand Rapids: Discovery House, 1995), 227.

CHAPTER 12: DO IT AGAIN

Claude Hickman, "Haystack Prayer Meeting," The Traveling Team, www.thetravelingteam.org/articles/haystack-prayer-meeting.

[2] Alicia Addison, "Luther Wishard," The Traveling Team, www.thetravelingteam.org/articles/luther-wishard?rq=wishard.

[3] Ibid.

APPENDIX

1 "Challenge 21 - 1998," YMCA International - World Alliance of YMCAs (World YMCA, September 25, 2020), https://www.ymca.int/about-us/ymca-history/challenge-21-1998/.

2 "Kampala Principles - 1973," YMCA International - World Alliance of YMCAs (World YMCA, June 1, 2020), https://www.ymca.int/about-us/ymca-history/kampala-principles-1973/.

BIBLIOGRAPHY

Addison, Alicia. "Luther Wishard." The Traveling Team. www.thetravelingteam.org/articles/luther-wishard?rq=wishard.

Binfield, J. C. G. *That Dear Man, George Williams, 1821–1905*. London: National Council of the YMCAs of England and Wales, 1970.

Birmingham Family YMCA. *Brick by Brick: Rebuilding Christian Emphasis in Your YMCA*. Birmingham, AL: Birmingham Family YMCA, 1992.

"Challenge 21—1998." YMCA International—World Alliance of YMCAs. World YMCA. www.ymca.int/about-us/ymca-history/challenge-21-1998/.

Chambers, Oswald, and James Reimann. *My Utmost for His Highest: Selections for Every Day*. Grand Rapids: Discovery House, 1995.

Chambers, Oswald. *He Shall Glorify Me: Talks on the Holy Spirit and Other Themes*. London: Oswald Chambers Publications Association and Christian Literature Crusade, 1975.

Dedmon, Emmett. *Great Enterprises: 100 Years of the YMCA of Metropolitan Chicago*. New York: Rand McNally, 1957.

Doggett, L. L., *History of the Young Men's Christian Association*, vol. 1. Cleveland: Imperial Press, 1896.

Dorsett, Lyle W. *A Passion for Souls: The Life of D. L. Moody*. Chicago: Moody Publishers, 2003.

Drummond, Lewis A. "The Secrets of Spurgeon's Preaching: Christian History Magazine." Christian History Institute, 1991. https://christianhistoryinstitute.org/magazine/article/secrets-of-spurgeon.

Encyclopedia of India Encyclopedia.com. www.encyclopedia.com/international/encyclopedias-almanacs-transcripts-and-maps/paul-k-t.

Engels, Frederick. *The Condition of the Working-Class in England in 1844 with a Preface Written in 1892* (version 17306). *Gutenburg.* The Project Gutenberg, 2005. www.gutenberg.org/files/17306/17306-h/17306-h.htm.

"The Funeral of Reverend Anthony Bowen." *Evening Star* (July 24, 1871). https://chroniclingamerica.loc.gov/lccn/sn83045462/1871-07-24/ed-1/seq-4/.

Global Ministries. "East Jerusalem YMCA (Palestine)." www.globalministries.org/partner/east_jerusalem_ymca/.

Haberman, Frederick W. "Nobel Lectures in Peace 1926–1950." *Nobel Lectures, 1926–1950.* World Scientific, 1999. https://doi.org/10.1142/3740.

Hallman, Tim. "Why the Walls Still Fall at the Jericho Y." Flourishing for All. March 4, 2020. www.timhallman.org/why-the-walls-still-fall-at-the-jericho-y/.

Hickman, Claude. "Haystack Prayer Meeting." The Traveling Team. www.thetravelingteam.org/articles/haystack-prayer-meeting.

Hillerbrand, Hans J. *The Encyclopedia of Protestantism*, vol. 4. Four vols. New York: Routledge, 2004.

Hopkins, C. Howard. "The Legacy of John R. Mott." *International Bulletin of Missionary Research* 5, no. 2 (1981): 70–73. https://doi.org/10.1177/239693938100500205.

Hopkins, Charles Howard. *History of the Y.M.C.A. in North America.* New York: Association Press, 1951.

"Inspire—Dictionary Definition." Vocabulary.com. www.vocabulary.com/dictionary/inspire.

Irving, George. "The Beginnings of Great Things." *The North American Student* 5, no. 1 (October 1916).

"Kampala Principles—1973." YMCA International—World Alliance of YMCAs. World YMCA. www.ymca.int/about-us/ymca-history/kampala-principles-1973/.

King, Martin Luther, Jr. "The Christian Pertinence of Eschatological Hope." The Martin Luther King, Jr., Research and Education Institute. Howard Gotlieb Archival Research Center, February 15, 1950. https://kinginstitute.stanford.edu/king-papers/documents/christian-pertinence-eschatological-hope.

Lewis, C. S. *Mere Christianity: A Revised and Amplified Edition, with a New Introduction, of the Three Books Broadcast Talks, Christian Behaviour, and Beyond Personality.* London: William Collins, 2017.

Limbert, Paul. *Christian Emphasis in YMCA Program.* New York: Association Press, 1944.

The Lord of the Rings: The Return of the King. Directed by Peter Jackson. Burbank, CA: New Line Cinema, 2003.

Lutzer, Erwin. "Totally Yielded to God." A Man for Our Times | Articles | Moody Church Media, 2014. www.moodymedia.org/articles/moody-man-our-times/.

MacKenzie, Ian. "Oral History and Stories—Peter Nasir." YMCA Heritage, 2019. https://ymcaheritage.com/wp-content/uploads/2020/04/Interview-with-Peter-Nasir-YMCA-Oral-Histories-and-Stories.pdf.

Matthews, Basil Joseph. *John R. Mott, World Citizen.* New York: Harper, 1934.

McCasland, Dave. *Oswald Chambers: Abandoned to God: The Life Story of the Author of My Utmost for His Highest.* Grand Rapids: Discovery House, 1993.

McCuaig, Donald. "James Naismith: Inventor of Basketball."
YMCA World 4 (December 2010).

"MetropolitanTabernacle." Charles Haddon Spurgeon's
Tabernacle—Metropolitan Tabernacle. www.metropolitantab-
ernacle.org/church-details/history.

Molebatsi, Caesar. "Reaching the Oppressed." *Transformation: An International Journal of Holistic Mission Studies* 7, no. 1 (1990): 25–27.
https://doi.org/10.1177/026537889000700110.

Moody, Dwight Lyman. *Pleasure and Profit in Bible Study*.
New York: Fleming H. Revell, 1895.

Moran, Ella V. "Anthony Bowen." *Negro History Bulletin* 8, no. 1 (1944):
5–21. www.jstor.org/stable/44214310.

Mott, John Raleigh. *Confronting Young Men with the Living Christ*. London:
Hodder and Stoughton, 1926.

Murray, Andrew. *Waiting on God: Daily Messages for a Month*.
Nabu Press, 2010.

"The Nobel Peace Prize 1946." NobelPrize.org, 2021.
www.nobelprize.org/prizes/peace/1946/summary/.

"Paris Basis—1855." YMCA International—World Alliance of
YMCAs. World YMCA, www.ymca.int/about-us/
ymca-history/paris-basis-1855/.

Parzany, Ulrich. "III. The Whole World: The Uniqueness of Christ II."
Lausanne Movement, October 19, 2018.
https://lausanne.org/content/manila-1989-documents.

"Plaque: YMCA." London Remembers. www.londonremembers.com/
memorials/ymca.

Mott, John R. "John R. Mott Letters." The Traveling Team.
www.thetravelingteam.org/articles/john-r-mott-letters.

Shedd, Clarence Prouty. *History of the World's Alliance of Young Men's Christian Associations*. 1st ed. London: S.P.C.K. for the World's Committee of Young Men's Christian Associations, 1955.

Tolkien., J. R. R. *The Fellowship of the Ring: Being the First Part of the Lord of the Rings*. New York: Del Rey, 2012.

Torrey, R. A. *Why God Used D. L. Moody*. New York: Fleming H. Revel, 1923.

Tozer, A. W. *The Pursuit of God: The Human Thirst for the Divine*. Chicago: Moody Publishers, 2015.

Welch, Tom. "James Naismith—Inventor of Basketball." YMCA Spiritual Legacy Series. Central Florida YMCA. https://s3.amazonaws.com/usmissionnetworkresources/Leadership/Legacy08+-+James+Naismith+%E2%80%93+Inventor+of+Basketball+-+USMN.pdf.

Welch, Tom. "Thomas Sullivan—Founder of the First YMCA in the United States." YMCA Spiritual Legacy Series. Central Florida YMCA. https://s3.amazonaws.com/usmissionnetworkresources/Leadership/legacy02+-+Capt.+Thomas+Sullivan+-+Founder+of +the+1st+YMCA+of+the+United+States+-+USMN.pdf.

Willard, Dallas. "Living in the Vision of God." https://dwillard.org/articles/living-in-the-vision-of-god.

Willems, Mo. *Goldilocks and the Three Dinosaurs*. New York: Balzer + Bray, 2012.

Williams, J. E. Hodder. *The Father of the Red Triangle: The Life of Sir George Williams, Founder of the Y.M.C.A.* London: Hodder and Stoughton, 1918.

Williams, J. E. Hodder. *The Life of Sir George Williams*. Cincinnati: Jennings and Graham, 1906.

Wilson, G. W., et al. *St.* Paul's *Cathedral & Blackfriars Bridge, London/ G.W.W. Library of Congress.* Library of Congress Prints and Photographs Division Washington, D.C. 20540 USA. www.loc.gov/resource/ppmsca.06814/.

Yancey, Philip. "God Behind Barbed Wire." *Christianity Today* (August 29, 2005). www.christianitytoday.com/ct/2005/september/20.120.html.

"YMCA History." YMCA International—World Alliance of YMCAs. World YMCA. www.ymca.int/about-us/ymca-history/.

YMCA of the USA. "YMCA Annual Pledge Statement." Chicago: unpublished internal document, 2007.

YMCA, Geneva. "Tribute to Henry Dunant: Founding Member of the World Alliance of YMCAs." *YMCA World* 4 (2010): 6–6.

"The Young Men of India," 1895., Box: 1. Kautz Family YMCA Archives.

Young Men's Christian Association. *Fifty Years' Work amongst Young Men in All Lands: A Review of the Work of the Young Men's Christian Associations.* London: Exeter Hall—Botolph Printing Works, 1894. https://hdl.handle.net/1813/29816.

Made in the USA
Coppell, TX
12 October 2021